MURRAY McMURRAY HATCHERY'S
CHICKENS IN FIVE MINUTES a DAY

MURRAY McMURRAY HATCHERY'S

CHICKENS iN FIVE MINUTES a DAY

Raising, Tending and Getting Eggs from a Small Backyard Flock MADE EASY

Murray McMurray Hatchery
selling chicks to people like you for nearly one hundred years

with April White

PAGE STREET
PUBLISHING CO.

PAGE STREET
PUBLISHING CO.

First published in the USA in 2013 by
Page Street Publishing Co.
27 Congress Street, Suite 205-10
Salem, MA 01970
www.pagestreetpublishing.com

Writer: April White

Distributed by Macmillan; sales in Canada by The Canadian Manda Group; distribution in Canada by The Jaguar Book Group.

16   15   14   13   1   2   3   4   5

ISBN-13: 978-1-62414-006-8

ISBN-10: 1-62414-006-8

Library of Congress Control Number: 2013931691

Cover and book design: Page Street Publishing Co.

Illustrations: Judy Love

Photography—Murray McMurray Hatchery: 50, 157; John Churchman: 47, 49, 51, 52, 53, 55, 57, 58, 145, 146, 147, 148, 149, 150, 151, 152; iStock: 44, 46, 53, 56, 58, 156, 158; Fotosearch: 55; Shutterstock: 44; Corbis: 55, 154, 159

Cover image: Kristi Harper

Printed and bound in United States of America

To Murray McMurray Hatchery's
customers-generations past, present
and future-for whom raising chickens
is a way to connect with their land,
their food and their families

Contents

chapter 1

WELCOME to the FLOCK

WHY RAISE CHICKENS?

Can't you just imagine a flock of chickens in your own backyard? Several sweet, golden-hued Buff Orpington hens, a few classic Rhode Island Reds and even some black-and-white Barred Rocks, all playing together and producing beautiful, fresh eggs for your breakfast table. It could be a reality in just five minutes a day, which is far less time than a trip to the grocery store for a dozen eggs.

OUR CHICKEN BACKYARD FARMING PHILOSOPHY

. . . .

At Murray McMurray Hatchery, we think everyone—and yes, that means you—can be a successful backyard chicken farmer. It isn't hard, as long as you start with healthy chicks. Your chickens will depend on you for food and water, and a safe, clean shelter. If you fulfill your part of the bargain, your chickens will fulfill theirs by producing eggs and providing endless entertainment for you and your family.

All you'll need is five minutes out of your day once you set up your backyard chicken coop properly. We speak from experience; at Murray McMurray Hatchery, we've been hatching and raising chickens for almost 100 years. Every year we ship millions of baby chicks to backyard chicken farmers around the country, just like you.

We have all different kinds of customers, from kids involved in 4-H projects; to home cooks who crave fresh eggs, to families who want fun, productive pets; to city dwellers who want a bit of the country in their lives. Even celebrities find time for a little backyard chicken farming; it's a relaxing break from performing and from paparazzi. On the wall in the hatchery are autographed pictures from backyard chicken farmers Martha Stewart, Bruce Springsteen and George Foreman, to name a few!

All our customers tell us the same thing: that backyard chicken farming is fun, easy, and very rewarding with a little advice from Murray McMurray. Yes, there's a lot to learn about raising chickens. But don't worry, once you learn the basics, your chickens will teach you the rest.

MURRAY MCMURRAY'S BUSINESS STARTED AS A BACKYARD FLOCK

Murray McMurray was a backyard chicken farmer, too. As a young man in the early 1900s, Murray raised a chicken flock for the same reasons that you are considering it, for fun and for delicious fresh eggs. Much to his delight, he also loved watching his flock interact and he most certainly loved showing his birds and winning ribbons at local fairs near his rural Iowa home.

When he grew up, Murray became a banker, but he never abandoned his chickens. Raising his flock was an easy, pleasant hobby during his banking days. He even began raising chicks and selling them to his banking peers, to other backyard farmers and even to large-scale chicken farms in Iowa. When the bank closed during the Great Depression, Murray went home and announced to his family that he was going to turn his backyard chicken farm into a business. That's how the Murray McMurray Hatchery got its start in an old gray house in downtown Webster City almost 100 years ago.

The Murray McMurray Hatchery continues to thrive in Webster City, but at a "new" hatchery on the outskirts of the city, where it's been for over twenty years. Here we hatch more than 2 million chicks a year and ship them to backyard chicken farmers throughout North America, backyard farmers who take the same joy in raising chickens that Murray did all those years ago.

Our humble beginnings and a deep love for chickens is what make our hatchery one of the greatest in the country.

HINTS FROM THE HATCHERY

CHRIS HUSEMAN

Years at Murray McMurray Hatchery: 1

Favorite breeds: Buff Orpington, Araucana/Americana and Red Star

"The task of raising chickens at first seemed daunting, especially because I didn't grow up on a farm. We only had a dog. I remember thinking, what are we getting into? But it's easy. The chickens just need food, water and shelter. That's it. They are so much fun to watch and the idea that you also get eggs from these girls is really amazing. The idea of raising chickens started with my daughter. She thinks they're funny, and they've been a way to introduce her to the idea of daily responsibility. They've been an educational tool and great pets."

WHY WE RAISE CHICKENS

We've been raising and selling chickens for a long time at Murray McMurray Hatchery and we've seen backyard chicken farming change a lot in those years. It seemed that during the '30s and '40s every household had a backyard flock to feed the family and make a little extra income from selling eggs, but by the '50s and '60s raising chickens was less popular. Fortunately, we're seeing a boom in backyard chicken farming as people all over the country, from farms in the Midwest to tiny backyards in Brooklyn, are getting excited about raising chickens.

We love chickens, and it's a good thing because every week from January through October, about 150,000 chicks are born in the incubators at the Murray McMurray Hatchery. That's a lot more chicks than ol' Murray McMurray ever dreamed of selling at the bank. It's a busy time for the hatchery staff. Within 72 hours, the chicks need to be counted, sorted, sexed, vaccinated, boxed and shipped to customers via the US Postal Service. The shipment of the chicks needs to happen quickly, while their bellies are still full of the egg yolk they ingested during hatching, to ensure that they arrive at their destination healthy, happy and cheeping.

▲ Raising chickens in your backyard can be fun and, yes, easy with a little advice from Murray McMurray Hatchery.

▲ Murray McMurray Hatchery has been supplying newly hatched chicks to backyard farmers like you for almost 100 years.

Hens raised by independent farmers around Webster City provide the eggs that we incubate and then hatch into tiny chicks that are so cute and fun that they're impossible not to love. We raise more than 100 different breeds and each has a unique job in the backyard farm. Some breeds are best for eggs, others for show, and others for pets, and all of them do their jobs well. We also raise some rare breeds that we are happy to reintroduce to backyard farms.

WHY YOU SHOULD RAISE CHICKENS

If you start talking to your friends, family and even mere acquaintances about chickens, you'll probably discover pretty quickly that you know lots of people who have a coop in their backyard or benefit from an overflow of fresh eggs from a neighbor's flock. You'll probably encounter even more people who are daydreaming about becoming backyard chicken farmers, just like you.

We don't have an accurate count of the number of backyard chicken farmers in the United States, but we do distribute millions of chicks each year to all 50 states. And we send out more chicks every year as interest in backyard chicken farming grows and people realize that even the smallest backyard can be home to a small, egg-producing flock. A flock of four chickens can be housed in six square feet (.56 square meters)!

CAN YOU RAISE CHICKENS IN YOUR NEIGHBORHOOD?

We think that backyard chicken farmers have a responsibility to their neighbors. This doesn't just mean giving away all those delicious eggs, though that's usually a much appreciated gesture. It also means ensuring that your chickens and their coop aren't a neighborhood nuisance. If your coop is dirty or is attracting pests or your chickens are feasting on the neighbor's flowers, you aren't doing your job as a backyard chicken farmer.

Although you may think of your chickens as pets, your community zoning laws might consider them livestock and have regulations on the books regulating, or even forbidding, raising chickens in your backyard. It's important to learn about your local laws before ordering your first flock. You can often find these regulations in your state or local municipal code (look for the information in the zoning, animal, health or nuisance codes) or through your local animal control office or extension agent.

Some zoning regulations limit the number of chickens per flock, set a minimum lot size, require a permit or dictate coop set-up. And they typically establish guidelines that are already standard among conscientious backyard farmers for clean and safe coops; the necessary space for chickens to live a healthy life; and rodent-proof feed storage. Regulations might also prohibit roosters, whose early morning cock-a-doodle-doos are frequently frowned upon by neighbors, and they might prohibit free-range chicken farming for fear of neighborhood property damage. Most community regulations prohibit the slaughter of chickens for meat.

However, there are more chicken-friendly communities than you might imagine. Even densely populated cities like Los Angeles, St. Louis and New York City allow backyard chicken farming. In fact, more than 80 percent of the country's most populated cities allow for backyard chicken farming in average size backyards. We've even found that ordinances restricting chickens are changing as would-be backyard chicken farmers educate their neighbors and elected officials about chickens. When properly cared for, chickens aren't smelly, noisy or bothersome; they are charming pets and efficient egg producers.

People just like you decide to start a backyard chicken farm for many different reasons. Some want a family project that provides the perfect opportunity to teach their children responsibility. Others fondly remember flocks in their parents', grandparents' and neighbors' backyards. Some entrepreneurial backyard farmers want extra income from the sale of eggs, and others simply want a unique–and yes, cuddly–pet.

Additionally, as people become more conscious and concerned about where their food comes from and how it has been handled, many want to raise chickens to produce eggs for their own consumption. When you raise your own chickens, you know the answers to important questions: Were the chickens raised in good conditions? Were they treated with antibiotics? Were the eggs handled and stored properly? As a backyard chicken farmer who's collecting the eggs, you know the answers.

▲ After you taste the fresh eggs from your backyard flock, you'll never want to eat supermarket eggs again.

Regardless of their reasons, backyard chicken farmers have two things in common, they love chickens and all of their silly antics and they know how easy it is to raise a healthy, happy flock. We are thrilled to see the joy and satisfaction of chicken farming continue in the tradition and honor of old Murray McMurray.

So, if you can picture yourself taking care of little chicks, just days old, and then you can picture mature chickens scratching in the yard, and, of course, if you can picture a daily trove of eggs, you're ready to become a backyard chicken farmer.

YOU CAN RAISE CHICKENS IN 5 MINUTES A DAY WITH THE MURRAY MCMURRAY METHOD

The key to becoming a backyard chicken farmer is good planning, both in setting up the chickens' coop and in your daily routine. Once you are set up, all you'll need is five minutes a day, and that's far less time than most other pets require! The Murray McMurray Method considers both the needs of the chickens and of the farmers.

With the Murray McMurray Method, the backyard chicken farmer has just a few responsibilities each day, a few minutes in the morning and then again at the end of the day. In a nutshell, you'll need to open the door to the chicken coop in the morning, to feed and water the chickens, to collect the eggs and to observe the chickens to be sure all their needs are met. In the evening, you'll close the door to the chicken coop. Once every month or two, as needed, you'll have to spend a little more time cleaning the coop. That's all it takes!

CHICKEN-FRIENDLY BIG CITIES

Of the country's ten most populous cities, eight are clearly chicken friendly. Crowded Philadelphia requires three acres (12141 square meters) of land to raise chickens, effectively prohibiting them. Houston also has large space requirements, but does allow up to seven chickens if a person presents a medical note testifying to his/her need for "fresh unfertilized chicken eggs for serious reasons pertaining to said person's health."

New York City
Allows hens

Los Angeles
Allows hens and roosters

Chicago
Allows hens

Phoenix
Allows up to 20 hens

San Diego
Allows up to 25 hens and roosters

Dallas
Allows hens and roosters, if roosters are confined

San Antonio
Allows up to three hens and roosters without a permit

San Jose
Allows up to six hens without a permit and up to 20 with a permit

The only flaw in the Murray McMurray Method is that it doesn't take into account how much time you'll spend enjoying your chickens. It's easy to get caught up in their antics and you might spend much more than five minutes a day watching them, but who would call that work?

So read on to learn how to set up a brooder for the baby chicks and a backyard coop for the chickens, how to tend to your chicks and chickens in just five minutes a day, and more about the different breeds of chickens. As a new farmer you will be amazed by how easy it is to be a very happy and efficient backyard chicken farmer, and current farmers might even learn a trick or two.

chapter 2

YOUR LIFE with CHICKENS

A DAY IN THE LIFE OF A BACKYARD CHICKEN FARMER

For many backyard chicken farmers, the word "chores" doesn't seem accurate. Tending to chickens isn't a job, but more of a hobby. It's a calming, daily routine, that can take as little as five minutes on busy or cold weekday mornings or can be stretched out and leisurely on a warm, lazy Sunday morning. When you have the time, nothing is more fun than watching and laughing at the dramas playing out between your hens in the chicken coop. Checking on the chickens is a perfect way to get children out of the house to breathe the fresh air. Chickens also add a rustic farm charm to your everyday life, no matter where you live.

THE JOY OF CHICKENS

Ask backyard chicken farmers why they love raising their chickens and, despite the many different reasons that people decide to have a flock, you'll likely get the same answer from all of them, that chicks and chickens are entertaining. It's as simple as that. You'll love watching the days-old cheeping chicks, tripping over each other and themselves as they race around the brooder. Then, they are just as entertaining as curious young chickens, as they are introduced to the wonders of the coop, and start scratching in the dirt, bathing enthusiastically in the dust and learning the routine of the backyard. They are even entertaining as mature hens, producing delicious eggs and strutting out to greet you each morning as you go about your daily chores.

And, of course, the standout bonus is their fresh eggs. They are creamy and rich tasting with their bright orange yolks. Here's a fair warning: you might not be able to eat a watery, pale-yellow store egg again, but you probably won't need to, either.

Chickens as Pets

Backyard chicken farmers often make the comparison between their flocks and Fido. Chickens aren't dogs, of course. You'll never put them on a leash and take them for a walk or train them to roll over, but they make great pets, nonetheless. Buff Orpington chickens, in particular, are often called the "Golden Retrievers of the chicken world." Chickens that are handled gently from the time they are chicks will enjoy interacting with humans. You can carry and cuddle a docile chicken, and some will even sit on your lap. Some chickens will learn to come to you when called by name, and most will clamor to see you every morning when you come to the coop, and not just because they know you're bringing food.

▲ Watching chickens interact is a favorite pastime of many backyard farmers. Think of it as "Chicken TV."

Pet chickens also require much less time than other pets. You can enjoy them whenever you want without feeling guilty if you need to ignore them, because they entertain themselves. No matter how well you train your other pets, they will never reward your care with a consistent source of fresh eggs, with rich, bright yolks for your breakfast or for sharing with friends.

IF YOU HAVE A DOG

Consider training your dog basic commands long before your chickens arrive.
If your dog is already used to taking direction from you, it will be easier to train him to leave the chicks alone. For more on how to introduce your dog to your chicks, see page 79.

▲ Chickens make great pets. You can carry and cuddle a hen, and some will learn to respond to their names.

▲ Raising backyard chickens is a fun family project. Kids will love collecting eggs each morning.

BECOMING A BACKYARD FARMER USING THE MURRAY MCMURRAY METHOD

Although it can seem intimidating, getting those eggs to your table isn't as hard as you think. Smart planning and a step-by-step guide (like this one) make it easy. If you've ever pictured yourself as a backyard chicken farmer, now's the time to become one.

A Seasonal Guide

This guide outlines the duties of a backyard chicken farmer from the fall when you order your chicks to the summer when you enjoy their eggs.

FALL: PLAN YOUR FLOCK AND ORDER YOUR CHICKS

It's important to plan your flock and order your chicks as soon as the hatchery catalog arrives in the fall or early winter. This will ensure that you get the breeds (see chapter 6) and delivery date you want in the spring. Many hatcheries sell out of chicks, especially the more popular breeds. You'll want your chicks to arrive in March, April or May because the chicks thrive in the warming weather and so do backyard chicken farmers!

WINTER: PREPARE FOR YOUR CHICKS

Use the colder months to prepare for your chicks (see chapters 4 and 5). Read up on their needs and purchase any supplies. You can make your own brooder and create your own run. You can even make your own coop, but you'll probably want to purchase a waterer, feeder and heat lamp.

EARLY SPRING: YOUR CHICKS ARRIVE!

Buy bedding and chick starter feed a week before your chicks are due to arrive. Pick a good spot and set up the brooder (see chapter 4). Pick up the chicks as soon as they arrive at the post office. Once home, dip their beaks in water, set them in the brooder and let the fun begin. Handle them gently and often. The more you and your family handle the chicks the friendlier they will be. Just wash your hands after each handling. Now you are a chicken farmer!

SUMMER: INTRODUCE YOUR CHICKENS TO THEIR COOP AND RUN

A week before you move the young chicks to the coop, buy adult feed, set up the coop, feeder and waterer, and put about two to three inches (5.1 to 7.6 cm) of bedding on the coop floor and in the nesting boxes (see chapter 5). Then, on a warmish day, put the chicks into the coop! It's an exciting moment for you and your adolescent chicks. At this point, you'll begin your five-minute daily routine of feeding, watering and observing your chickens. You might also want to start collecting egg cartons from friends and family.

LATE SUMMER: COLLECT THE EGGS

Depending on the breed, your chicks will begin laying eggs between the ages of four and seven months. That first egg is really special, small and usually soft (but don't eat it). Your chickens will continue to produce eggs and be endearing, entertaining pets for many years to come. It's as easy as that.

A Daily Guide

You'll start your day by heading to the chicken coop with some kitchen scraps to treat your birds. Open the coop door to let your chickens into the run and toss the kitchen scraps into the run. Add fresh water to the waterer from the hose or a bucket and fill the feeder with a scoop of chicken feed (see page 121 for water and feed supply locations). Collect the eggs from the nesting boxes, which hopefully open toward the outside of the coop to make egg collection easier (see page 135). Add a scoop of bedding to the nesting boxes from the container nearby. And, with all your extra time, watch the chickens explore the run before returning to the house to wash and sort the eggs.

With the Murray McMurray Method, your chicken chores only require five minutes a day unless you get distracted playing with these personable birds. Plan to visit your chickens for a few minutes each morning.

WATERING

Your chickens need access to clean water every day. A waterer and a hose or a bucket system makes it quick and easy to replace the water in the coop and run (see page 117).

FEEDING

A balanced chicken feed that is stored in pest-proof containers and housed near the coop for easy access is the everyday staple of your chickens' diet (see page 113). As a treat, the birds will also enjoy fresh kitchen scraps tossed into their run. Don't overdo it with kitchen scraps or particularly fragrant foods to avoid attracting predators.

8. Return to the house to sort and store eggs.

1. Head to the coop with some kitchen scraps to treat your birds.

4. Fill the feeder with a scoop of chicken feed.

3. Add fresh water to the waterer.

7. Observe and enjoy your chickens.

A DAY IN THE LIFE OF
A BACKYARD CHICKEN FARMER

5. Collect the eggs.

6. Add more bedding to the nesting boxes to replace any kicked out by the hens.

2. Open the coop door, tossing the kitchen scraps into the run.

COLLECTING

When your chickens start laying eggs, you should check the nesting boxes in the coop at least once a day for fresh eggs. When you check for eggs, add a scoop of bedding to each nesting box. The new bedding provides a clean resting place for the chickens and the eggs and absorbs the contents of any broken eggs.

OBSERVING

Watching your chickens interact can provide hours of entertainment, but observing changes in behavior is also important for your chickens' health. Good backyard farmers get to know their chickens and can spot lethargy, loss of appetite and other symptoms that might be the first signs of illness.

A Monthly Guide

CLEANING THE COOP

A well-designed coop and run and a little daily maintenance make this chore easier. For the sake of your birds' health and your relationship with your neighbors, who are unlikely to appreciate barnyard aromas, the coop needs to be cleaned whenever it's heavily soiled or smells like ammonia, usually every one to two months (see page 138).

HINTS FROM THE HATCHERY

DEBBIE JAYCOX

Years at Murray McMurray Hatchery: 26

Favorite breeds: Belgian Bearded d'Uccle Mille Fleur, Cochin and Partridge Rock

"I started on the phones here at the hatchery. That's where I learned everything I know about chickens. There's a great community of poultry enthusiasts, and with blogs and Twitter and Facebook there's more interaction in the community than ever. If I can give people one word of advice, it's to observe. Observe your chickens. The chickens will tell you what they want. Are they huddling by the heat lamp? Are they eating? Are they active? If you watch your birds, they are telling you in their own way what they need."

chapter 3

CHOOSING YOUR CHICKENS

CONSIDER YOUR GOALS AND THE DESIRED SIZE OF YOUR FLOCK

There are two key questions you should consider as you daydream about your new flock: how many birds will you raise and what is your primary goal in raising chickens?

THE RIGHT-SIZED FLOCK FOR YOUR BACKYARD

How many chickens can you raise in your backyard? The general rule of thumb is that each standard-size chicken requires 1 ½ to 2 square feet (.138 to .185 square meters) of space in the coop. That's not a lot of space!

- For a flock of 4, you'll need 6 to 8 square feet (.58 to .74 square meters)
- For a flock of 6, you'll need 9 to 12 square feet (.84 to 1.11 square meters)
- For a flock of 12, you'll need 18 to 24 square feet (1.67 to 2.23 square meters)
- For a flock of 20, you'll need 30 to 40 square feet (2.79 to 3.72 square meters)

You can certainly raise just one chicken, but chickens are social creatures and you'll end up acting as your chicken's flock. Be prepared to spend a lot of time interacting with your solo chicken. Plus, you'll need all the same equipment to raise one chicken, so why not raise four or six? Chicks aren't expensive, just a few dollars apiece, so it makes more sense to start with a flock of at least four chicks.

Of course, most hatcheries have a minimum order of chicks, which is typically 15 to 25. There's safety and warmth in numbers while the birds are in transit. If a flock of 15 is too many for your backyard, consider sharing an order with a friend or using an online message board to find other backyard chicken farmers in your area to split the order.

Some hatcheries also sell a small selection of started chickens that are brooded at the hatchery. These chickens are delivered to you at 15 to 22 weeks old, just a few weeks before they start laying eggs. You miss the fun of day-old chicks, but you can order just one or two started chickens.

MINI-GLOSSARY OF CHICKEN TERMINOLOGY

Bantam

Miniature chicken breeds that are typically less than half the size of standard breeds (some bantam breeds are miniature versions of standard breeds, while others come in the diminutive size only)

Chick

A young chicken, typically up to about six weeks old

Cockerel

A young male chicken, typically less than one year old

Hen

A mature female chicken

Rooster

A mature male chicken

Pullet

A young female chicken, typically less than one year old

Sexing

Sexing is the act of determining the sex of a newly hatched chick. This can be difficult to do in some breeds. Hatcheries typically guarantee 90 percent accuracy and have specially trained and licensed people to identify the gender.

Sex linked

A chick that can be sexed by color at the time of hatching

Standard

Breeds of chickens in which the average hen is 4 ½ pounds (2 kg) for light breeds to 8 ½ pounds (3.85 kg) for heavy breeds

Started chickens

Chickens that are brooded at the hatchery and are delivered to you at 15 to 22 weeks old, just a few weeks before they start laying eggs

Straight run

An order of chicks that hasn't been sorted by sex

Small Space Options

A good option when you have limited space is bantam chickens. Bantams are less than half the size of standard chickens at maturity and require half the space. Bantam and standard breeds can co-exist in a flock, just watch out that the smaller bantams aren't being bullied in the coop.

Bantams are also less than half the size of standard chickens at birth; some are no bigger than your thumb as newly hatched chicks. Their eggs, too, are under half the size, so while they are just as delicious as the eggs you'll collect from standard birds, you do need at least twice as many to make your morning omelet.

White Silkie Bantam

Buff Cochin

WHICH CHICKENS ARE BEST FOR YOU AND YOUR LOCATION

Once you've decided how many chickens you want, your breed choices will be dictated by your reasons for raising chickens, the climate you live in and your own personal preferences.

Hatchery catalogs are hard to resist with all the intriguing breeds from which to choose. The Murray McMurray Hatchery offers more than 100 different breeds each season so the choices can seem overwhelming. Don't worry; choosing is more art than science once you determine your goals. You can easily mix and match breeds to create your own unique backyard flock. It's not recommended, however, to mix chickens with other types of fowl, and it can be difficult to integrate new chicks with your older flock (see page 91).

Consider your primary reasons for raising chickens. Is it for egg production, in which case do you want white eggs, brown eggs or multi-colored eggs? Do you care what your chickens look like? Are you looking for docile chickens that make good pets, or more alert birds suitable for free-ranging? And do you live in a very warm or very cool climate?

Egg Production

Although there is no difference in taste between white, brown and multi-colored eggs, many people have a preference. The color comes from a pigment secreted by the hen as the egg is laid. A chicken will lay the same color egg all her life, though the depth of the color may change with age. For a glossary of chicken breeds, see chapter 6.

IF YOU WANT A LOT OF WHITE EGGS

If ample white-egg production is your top priority, you'll want a flock of Pearl-White Leghorns, an Easter-yellow chick that grows into a tall white egg-laying machine. If you prefer a mixed flock with high white-egg production, add graceful Silver Spangled Hamburgs, lively Single Comb Brown Leghorns or proud Blue Andalusians (only 50 percent of which, thanks to genetics, are actually blue).

Pearl-White Leghorn

Blue Andalusian

Silver Spangled Hamburg

Single Comb Brown Leghorn

HINTS FROM THE HATCHERY

BUD WOOD

Years at Murray McMurray Hatchery: 12

Favorite breeds: Red Star, Rhode Island Red and Barred Rock

"There are no right or wrong answers for choosing the best breed for you. It's a personal choice. The best way to choose the right breed is to make a list of what you want in a chicken and prioritize each characteristic. My personal list includes: large brown-egg layers, good egg producers, birds with quiet temperaments and birds with interesting colors and patterns on their plumage. That last one is low on my list, but my daughters usually move it to the top. As you can see, my favorite birds are high producing, brown-egg layers. Some of my favorites in the category are Red Stars, Rhode Island Reds and Barred Rocks. Make your own list and have fun looking through our catalog or website to find the breeds that meet your needs."

DO YOU WANT A ROOSTER?

First things first: you don't need a rooster for your hens to produce eggs or to protect your flock. Your small flock of hens will produce delicious (unfertilized) eggs without a rooster in the coop, and a secure coop and run will keep your chickens safe from predators without a rooster acting as watchdog over the flock.

Some backyard chicken farmers like keeping roosters as well as hens. For early-risers, a rooster's sunrise crowing can be a pleasant, even soothing sound, and many breeds of roosters are beautiful and colorful. But some neighbors and communities view roosters as noisy and aggressive so be sure to check your zoning laws before adding a rooster to your backyard. For these reasons, most backyard chicken farmers choose to raise only hens.

Single Comb Brown Leghorn Rooster

IF YOU WANT A LOT OF BROWN EGGS

You'll get the highest production of large, brown eggs from easy-to-raise Red Stars and Black Stars. If you want to diversify your flock, you can add other good brown-egg layers like the well-known Rhode Island Reds, the stately Buff Orpingtons and the cold-hardy Barred Rocks.

Red Star

Black Star

Rhode Island Red

Barred Rock

Buff Orpington

IF YOU WANT MULTI-COLORED EGGS

If you want the "Easter egg" chicken, then choose Araucana/Americanas, whose show-and-tell-worthy eggs vary in shades from turquoise to jade to olive. Each hen lays the same shade throughout her life, even though the saturation of the color dims with age. As with the white and brown eggs, the color of the egg shell doesn't affect the taste or color of the egg yolk and white. The birds themselves also come in a wide assortment of colors and patterns, making for a unique flock. You can combine a white-egg-laying Pearl-White Leghorn, a brown-egg-laying Red Star or Black Star and a Cuckoo Maran that lays chocolate brown eggs for even more egg color variety.

Arucana/Americana

Arucana/Americana

Arucana/Americana

Arucana/Americana

Arucana/Americana

Appearance

Different chicken breeds have different and distinctive appearances. Feathers can be white, red, brown, black, gold, and even blue. Some chickens have spots and some have stripes. Some even have curls (the Frizzle Cochins). There are breeds with majestic crests and breeds with sleek heads. There are breeds with long tails and breeds with no tail at all. For the most part, these differences in appearances are merely cosmetic. Most chickens that are raised together, even of different breeds, get along together despite the physical differences, but sometimes chickens with particularly brilliant plumage may get pecked at by other chickens in the flock (see page 169 for solving this problem).

IF YOU WANT EXOTIC-LOOKING BIRDS

Although there are many interesting breeds, backyard farmers who take pride in raising exotic birds often turn to bantams. Little is known about the origin of these miniature birds, but their beautiful coloring is well appreciated.

If you want a bright, active flock, consider blue-skinned White Silkies, Blue Silkies (half the chicks will grown into blue birds; the others will be black and/or white), Frizzle Cochins (three-quarters of the fuzzy chicks will grow into frizzled chickens), heavily-feathered Belgian Bearded d'Uccle Mille Fleurs and bearded Quail Antwerp Belgians.

Frizzled Cochin

Mille Fleur Rooster

Quail Antwerp Belgian

White Silkie

As a fair warning, because of their miniature size, most hatcheries don't sex bantams at birth. This means that if a backyard bantam farmer orders a "straight run" of bantams the flock will, on average, be half male and half female. So only choose this path if you want a rooster (see page 42)!

Temperament

All chicken breeds can make good pets, especially if you spend time with them, handle them gently, and teach young children and any other visitors around your backyard farm how to interact with them. Of course, an individual bird within a breed can develop a personality distinct from the breed's expected nature. Silver Spangled Hamburgs, for instance, are known for being flighty and alert (a great quality for free-range birds), but you might find you have a calm and quiet one.

Buff Orpington

Still, there are breeds that are a better choice when you want your chickens to be family-friendly first and egg producers second. For this scenario, you might consider gentle Cochins and quiet Orpingtons. Both are average layers with strong mothering instincts. You'll be able to pick these breeds up and hold them and still get plenty of eggs.

If you're considering showing your pet birds, which is a 4-H project that many kids love, order multiple birds of the same breed. Some chickens in your flock will show better than others of the same breed. There is always variation among the physical characteristics within the breed and some chickens will simply have a better temperament for competition.

Black Cochin

Silver-Laced Cochin

Partridge Cochin Hens

Location

Most chicken breeds can survive and thrive in all the different climates of the United States, but some are definitely more suited to particular climates.

IF YOU LIVE IN A COLD CLIMATE

Most chickens are hardy enough to thrive through the winter in colder climates as long as they have appropriate housing. However some breeds are better equipped for cold weather than others. Breeds are divided into "light" and "heavy" categories. "Light" hens have a mature weight of four to seven pounds (1.8 to 3.17 kg) and are not as capable as heavier chickens of staying warm in cold weather. "Heavy" chickens have a mature weight of seven to nine pounds (3.17 to 4.08 kg) and can easily keep themselves warm in the cold winter months.

GOOD BREEDS FOR COLD WEATHER:

- Cochin
- Orpington
- Plymouth Rock
- Rhode Island
- Star
- Silkie

Besides weight, breeds with a short comb or a rose comb are also better suited to colder climates than breeds with a long single comb because the long single comb is particularly susceptible to freezing in cold temperature. If the comb does freeze, it must be thawed and the chicken will likely stop laying eggs for a while. Some backyard farmers also prefer clean-legged breeds in cold-weather climates. Snowy weather and a slushy spring can make a mess of leg feathers.

IF YOU LIVE IN A WARM OR HOT CLIMATE

Most chickens thrive in hot weather as long as water and shade are available and the coop is well ventilated (it's a bad sign if your chickens are panting like a dog). Light breeds are more tolerant of the heat, and lighter-color feathers absorb less heat from the sun. Black-feathered breeds overheat more easily and fare better in less tropical climates.

GOOD BREEDS FOR WARM WEATHER:

- Araucana/Americana
- Blue Andalusian
- Hamburg
- Leghorn
- Quail Antwerp Belgian

ORDERING YOUR CHICKS

If you're still not sure which breed to order, refer to the glossary of breeds in chapter 6. Some people are drawn to what they perceive as a traditional chicken, like what grandma had, maybe Pearl-White Leghorns or Rhode Island Reds. Others choose chickens they've seen in their friends' backyard flocks. Breeds like Buff Orpington and Red Star are currently popular. And the chicken on the cover of the hatchery catalog is always a big seller. Remember, hatchery catalogs come out in the late fall or early winter and experienced backyard chicken farmers place their chick orders quickly to ensure that they get their first choice of breeds and delivery date, so act fast.

If you don't want to design your own flock, most hatcheries sell an assorted flock that fulfills a specific purpose, like an assortment of brown-egg layers. The hatchery chooses the breeds based on availability, and you save a little money.

Time to Order

Once you've chosen the breed of chickens you want to order, there are still a few decisions to make.

WHEN DO YOU WANT YOUR CHICKENS TO ARRIVE?

At Murray McMurray Hatchery, chicks start hatching in late January. Every week, a new flock hatches and within hours the newly hatched birds are on their way to their new owners. Within 72 hours they will be at your local post office, in need of your prompt attention and care. When placing an order date, consider the spring temperatures in your region and whether it stays cold late into the season. If so, pick a later hatch date for the well-being of your chicks.

Your chicks will be just days old when they arrive at your local post office and will travel in a box designed to make their trip as comfortable as possible. In warmer months, the box may be dotted with ventilation holes to keep the birds cool. In colder months, the box may be lined with heating pads to warm the little birds. And they will be nourished during their trip by the egg yolk that they ingest during hatching.

DO YOU WANT YOUR CHICKENS VACCINATED?

Most backyard chicken farmers choose to have their day-old chicks vaccinated at the hatchery to protect them from Marek's disease and Coccidiosis. These vaccines are best given in the first three days of life. Marek's disease, which can't be treated, can cause paralysis and death in young chickens. Coccidiosis is an infection of intestinal parasites that also causes death among young birds. It can be prevented by vaccination or through medicated chick feed. Although the medicated feed passes from the system before the chicks reach egg-laying age, some farmers prefer the vaccination to reduce the amount of time medication is given to the chickens. If the vaccination is given at the hatchery, do not give your chicks medicated feed because it will counteract the effects. Vaccinated chicks are still considered organic under nationally recognized guidelines.

DO YOU WANT SUBSTITUTIONS?

How committed are you to your breed choices? You'll be asked if substituting a similar breed is okay if your first choice isn't available. You can often request a second choice or similar characteristics. Being flexible is a good characteristic for a backyard chicken farmer; this is nature, after all.

DO YOU WANT EXTRA CHICKS?

Some hatcheries will add extra chicks to a shipment on cold days and Murray McMurray Hatchery offers a free rare chick with each chick order. Some backyard farmers who know exactly what breeds they want in their flock or worry about getting a rooster decline these extra birds.

ARE YOU PREPARED FOR THE ARRIVAL OF YOUR CHICKS?

Read on for everything you need to know to raise your new chicks in five minutes a day with the Murray McMurray Method.

chapter 4

THE MURRAY MCMURRAY METHOD for RAISING NEWLY HATCHED CHICKS in FIVE MINUTES a DAY

EVERYTHING YOU NEED TO KNOW FOR THOSE FIRST FEW WEEKS

Be well prepared for the arrival of your newly hatched chicks. They will be entirely dependent on you to keep them safe, warm, clean and well fed, but caring for your new flock will be easy if you plan ahead and have the right equipment and supplies on hand.

GETTING READY

Your chicks will be arriving soon! As their arrival date grows closer, you may feel a little like an expectant parent, incredibly excited and more than a little nervous. You might find yourself daydreaming about the playful young birds and the fun you'll have watching and interacting with them. You might also wonder if you are ready to take care of the little dependent chicks. Don't worry, this chapter helps you set up for the delivery of your new chicks and then care for them during the first weeks of their lives.

For the first four to six weeks of their lives, your chicks will hop, play, eat and drink in a brooder, which is a warm, safe home with soft bedding, fresh water and ample food. It is typically located in your home, barn, or garage, where the young chicks are safe from predators. About a week or two before their scheduled arrival, you should build a simple brooder and stock up on feed and nutritional supplements formulated specifically for chicks. Think of it like preparing a nursery for an infant. When your birds arrive, cheeping loudly, they'll have their first home and you'll be ready to care for them. You and your chicks will quickly settle into a daily routine.

THE NEW CHICK SUPPLY CHECKLIST

These are the supplies you'll need to have ready for the arrival of your chicks. You should have these on hand one to two weeks before the chicks are to arrive. The items are further described in this chapter.

- Brooder: About $8

- Bedding: About $6 for a big bale

- Newspaper, large enough to cover the floor of the brooder

- 1 one-quart (.95 liter) chick waterer: About $5

- Chick feeder with 2 ½ to 3 inches (6.4 to 7.6 cm) of space per chick: About $4

- 1 250-watt red heat lamp: About $27

- Easy-to-read thermometer: About $3

- Digital thermometer: About $20

- White sugar

- 1 package probiotic gel: About $4

- Hand sanitizer

The following items are enough for a flock of 12 for about 4 weeks:

- 1 four-ounce (113.4 grams) package of Quik Chik, a vitamin-electrolyte mix: About $5

- 1 five-pound (2.27 kg) bag of chick starter feed: About $6

- 1 five-pound (2.27 kg) bag of chick grit (even the smallest bag of grit is far more than you will need): About $10

SETTING UP THE BROODER

A brooder isn't anything fancy; it's merely a temporary and expandable home to keep your chicks contained and safe from drafts and predators. We recommend a 12-inch (30.5 cm) wide length of cardboard that you can staple together to the desired diameter (see below) and rest on a bed of newspaper and bedding. The circular shape is important because there are no corners for panicked or cold chicks to crowd into and potentially suffocate under other birds. To the brooder, you'll add a chick waterer, a chick feeder and a heat lamp to satisfy the needs of all your chicks.

The diameter of the brooder is important and it will need to expand as the chicks grow. Plan for at least ½ square foot (.15 square meter) per newly hatched chick, so six newly hatched chicks need a brooder at least 2 feet (61 cm) in diameter; and 12 chicks need a brooder at least 3 feet (92 cm) in diameter. By the time your chicks are four weeks old, they will each need about ¾ square foot (.23 square meter), or a brooder 2 ½ feet (76 cm) in diameter for six chicks and about 3 ½ feet (107 cm) for 12 chicks.

At four weeks, your chicks will begin to outgrow the brooder in other ways. Your rambunctious four-week-olds will learn to fly over brooder walls. This is funny, until you realize what a mess they can make. If the weather in your area is warm enough, it might be time to transition your flock to their coop. If it's still chilly outside or if your chicks haven't developed their feathers yet, you can raise the height of the walls and lay a screen over the brooder. A good test to determine if it's warm enough to move them to the coop is to ask yourself whether you would sleep out there in a light sleeping bag.

A SIMPLE BROODER

Brooder: A round brooder prevents the chicks from bunching up in the corners.

Newspaper: To line the bottom of the brooder and protect your floor.

Bedding: Coarse bedding, like pine shavings, which the birds won't mistake for food, placed on top of the newspaper makes for simple clean up.

Feeder and waterer: These supplies are necessary to ensure that your chicks have food and water. Be sure there is enough room at the feeder and water for all your chicks.

Heat lamp: Necessary to maintain the right temperature for your chicks. You can adjust the height of the heat lamp to control the temperature in the brooder.

Brooder Location

Choose a safe, warm and convenient location for the brooder. While we understand owners may choose to brood chickens in their houses, the U.S. Centers of Disease Control and Prevention strongly suggests against this. Wherever you choose to brood your chicks, it should be an area protected from predators, including family pets and unsupervised children, at least until the chicks are older. The location should have enough space to store extra feed and bedding for easy maintenance.

◂ A simple brooder made from cardboard and newspaper will be your chicks' home for their first weeks.

It should also be a draft-free area where the temperature is constant. It's not just the air temperature that's important. Check the ground temperature, too. If it's cold to the touch, it will rob precious heat from your birds. If the brooder is on concrete, for example, you should place plywood under the brooder to insulate the chicks.

During the first few weeks of your life as a backyard chicken farmer, you'll visit your chicks often, so, if possible, put the brooder somewhere where you're comfortable, too.

Perfect Bedding

There are three types of bedding that aren't suitable for your brooder. First, it shouldn't be too fine; you need bedding coarse enough that the chicks won't mistake their bedding for food, which is why sawdust is a bad idea. Second, you want something that's easy for you to clean, which is why straw is a bad idea. Third, you should never use cedar or treated wood chips because the oils and off-gases are highly toxic to chicks, so they are clearly a bad idea.

As long as you don't use sawdust, straw or treated wood chips, the type of bedding you choose depends on where you live. Any coarse organic material will work. Pine shavings are the most common and tend to be available throughout the country, but in some regions you'll see rice hulls or ground corncobs used successfully as bedding.

Before you put the bedding in the brooder, line the brooder with newspaper for easy cleanup. Add bedding to the brooder until it's 1-inch (2.5 cm) thick.

Easy-fill Waterer

A chick waterer ensures that your chicks always have access to water and that they don't make too much of a mess with it. A waterer comes in two parts, a jar that holds the water and a base that releases the water slowly into a narrow trough around the rim. Your chicks will gather around the rim so they need plenty of room. A one-quart waterer (.95 liter) is large enough for up to 12 chicks to drink at the same time.

Don't be tempted to put a bowl of water in your brooder. Your new chicks will get all wet trying to drink from the bowl, and a wet chick can become dangerously cold.

If the bedding gets into and clogs the waterer as the chicks scamper around, you can raise the waterer an inch (2.5 cm) off the ground with a small piece of wood or another prop. Just make sure the birds can still drink easily.

▲ An easy-to-fill waterer provides a steady supply of water for your young flock. The narrow trough helps prevent the birds from playing in the water.

Simple Feeder

A chick feeder is another simple device. It sometimes looks like a waterer, with a jar that holds the food and a base where the food collects, or it can be a simple trough. The trick is to have enough space for your chicks to feed. You don't want the less aggressive chicks to miss out on dinner. You'll need about 1 inch (2.5 cm) of space per newly hatched chick, either in a line at a trough or around a circular feeder. But plan ahead because your four-week-old chicks will need 2 ½ to 3 inches (6.4 to 7.6 cm) of space each before they move out into their coop.

Heat Lamp

A hanging and adjustable heat lamp with a 250-watt red heat bulb should be the centerpiece of your brooder. Position it above the middle of the brooder, about 18 inches (45.7 cm) above the bedding. You'll need to be able to adjust the height of the lamp over time to change the temperature of the brooder.

Be sure to turn the heat lamp on 12 to 24 hours before you get your chicks so they have a nice warm landing pad. Day-old chicks, covered with downy fluff, need summer-like temperatures between 90°F–95°F (32°C–35°C). Use your thermometer to double check the temperature periodically. Five-week-old chicks, covered with feathers, need early spring-like temperatures around 70°F (21°C). The chicks will also regulate their own temperature by moving closer to the center of the brooder for more heat and toward the edges for less. Make sure the heat lamp doesn't illuminate and heat the entire brooder, the edges should be darker and cooler than the center.

▲ Simple feeders come in different shapes. Just be sure your birds all have room to eat.

CARING FOR YOUR NEWLY HATCHED CHICKS

Hatcheries make every effort to ensure that all the chicks arrive safely, but there is the unfortunate possibility a chick might die in transit so parents should consider opening the box to ensure that the chicks all survived the journey before showing the box to children.

▲ Chicks from Murray McMurray Hatchery will arrive at the post office in a cardboard box. They will probably be cheeping loudly and healthily.

When They First Arrive

When your chicks arrive, they will be very cute and quite boisterous, cheeping loudly for your attention. Don't get too distracted by their antics as they are hungry and thirsty. Your first task as a backyard chicken farmer is to introduce your new chicks to their brooder and help them find food, water and warmth.

It is important to leave the chicks in the box and introduce them into the brooder one at a time as follows.

- Introduce your baby birds to their water right away; not drinking is the leading cause of death among newly hatched chicks. Mix one quart (.95 liter) of warm, but not hot, water with 3 tablespoons (45 ml) of white sugar. You should also add Quik Chik, a vitamin-electrolyte mix, according to the instructions on the

▼ Your first official act as a backyard chicken farmer is introducing the chicks to water one by one.

package. Measure carefully; there is a lot of salt in Quik Chik and too much salt can be toxic to chicks. Fill the waterer with the solution. Now gently take one chick at a time out of the box and dip its beak into the water before letting it loose. If, later, you see any chicks acting lethargic or wobbly, try dipping their beaks in the water again.

• Fill the feeder with a starter feed specially formulated for chicks with an 18% protein level. If you chose to have your chicks vaccinated for Coccidiosis at the hatchery (see page 62), choose non-medicated feed. If the chicks were not vaccinated, choose a medicated feed to prevent Coccidiosis.

  If the chicks try to eat their bedding instead of their food, change the bedding so it is larger and coarser. You can also cover the bedding with an old t-shirt and sprinkle some food on top of it to ensure that the chicks find the food easily. Another option is to place a sheet pan sprinkled with food in the brooder on top of the bedding. Covering the bedding with newspaper isn't recommended because newspaper is slick, and the fragile chicks may injure themselves sliding on it. You can remove the t-shirt or pan when the chicks start finding their food.

• Newly arrived chicks also benefit from probiotics, which will populate their digestive system with healthy bacteria. Mix a package of probiotic gel with water according to the package instructions and spread the bright green gel over the chicks' food. As they eat the gel supplement, your birds will get water, proteins, amino acids, carbohydrates, fats, vitamins and probiotic bacteria, all important for healthy chicks. Remove and dispose of any remaining probiotic gel after 24 hours.

This is the start of your new routine, providing fresh water with Quik Chik and feed to your chicks each morning and evening and ensuring that they are safe and warm.

On the third day, begin to add baby grit to the feed. Grit is tiny, rough rocks that help the birds digest their food. The baby version is much finer than the adult version. Sprinkle the grit on the feed as if you were salting food. Be careful not to add too much or the birds will fill up on the grit. Stop adding white sugar to the Quik Chik-fortified water on the third day.

Introduce your dog to your chicks shortly after they arrive and with your supervision. Some backyard chicken farmers who are also dog owners suggest first familiarizing your dog with the scent of the chicks by lightly rubbing a cloth on the chicks and placing the scented cloth in the dog bed. Then interact with the dog while handling the chicks, allowing the dog to sniff the now-familiar scent. Reinforce basic commands for the dog to leave the chickens alone and reward good behavior. Continue the training when the chickens are transferred to the coop.

THE MURRAY MCMURRAY METHOD
FIVE-MINUTE ROUTINE: THE FIRST THREE DAYS

Day One

Brooder temperature: 90°F–95°F (32°C–35°C)

Water: Mix 3 tablespoons (45 ml) of white sugar with one quart (.95 liter) of water, fortified with Quik Chik to give your chicks extra energy. Dip each chick's beak in the water before releasing it into the brooder; this will help the chick find the water. Change the water twice daily.

Feed: Fill the chick feeder with chick starter feed and spread probiotic gel on top of the feed. You can also cover the brooder's bedding with an old t-shirt or a sheet pan and spread some feed on top. This will help your chicks find the feed instead of trying to eat the bedding.

Day Two

Brooder temperature: Maintain at 90°F–95°F (32°C–35°C)

Water: Continue to add 3 tablespoons (45 ml) of white sugar to each quart (.95 liter) of water fortified with Quik Chik. Change the water twice daily.

Feed: Keep the feeders filled. Remove any remaining probiotic gel.

Day Three

Brooder temperature: Maintain at 90°F–95°F (32°C–35°C)

Water: It's no longer necessary to add white sugar to the water fortified with Quik Chik. Continue to change the water twice daily. Never let your birds run out of water.

Feed: Keep the feeders filled. Begin sprinkling feed with baby grit as if you were salting food.

WHAT TO WATCH FOR

Your chicks will let you know that you're off to a good start as a backyard chicken farmer. Healthy, happy chicks will run around the brooder like children in a playground. Your chicks will also let you know when they aren't feeling well. Watch for signs that your chicks need a little extra care. Reintroduce water and food to any weak-looking chicks by dipping their beaks in the water and putting their beaks near the food a number of times.

LETHARGY

If your birds appear to have had a particularly hard journey, if their eyes aren't open or their heads are droopy, you can help them recover by adding 6 tablespoons (95 ml) of white sugar to their one quart (.95 ml) of water for the first three or four days. You should also mix this extra-sweet water with the feed to create a soupy mixture for your birds for the first three or four days.

PASTING UP

The stress of travel can cause loose stool. This can "paste up" on the chicken's feathers around their anus. While an unpleasant job, you must remove this daily, as it can block elimination. If there is manure on a chick, wash it off gently with a cloth and warm water. The condition should pass in a couple of days.

▲ Your chicks' behavior will tell you if the brooder is too cold or too warm, but a thermometer is also a helpful tool for the backyard chicken farmer to double check the correct temperature.

HUDDLING

If your chicks are huddling together directly under the heat lamp, the brooder probably isn't warm enough. Use your thermometer to measure the temperature under the lamp and lower the lamp to increase the heat. On the other hand, if the chicks are all at the margins of the brooder, well away from the heat lamp, the brooder may be too hot. You can raise the lamp to reduce the heat. In a well-heated brooder, chicks will often form a circle around the heat lamp, absorbing the warmth at the edges of light.

PECKING

Your chicks may peck at each other, injuring one another, or even themselves with their beaks. Some of this is the natural establishment of a pecking order (see page 169), but aggressive behavior and bullying can lead quickly to injury.

It's important to correct this behavior and treat the injured birds promptly. Chicks may peck because they are crowded or too hot. Check that the size of your brooder and that the output of your heat source is appropriate. Bright light can also cause pecking. That's why red, not white, heat lamps are recommended. Try darkening the room to discourage pecking. Your chicks might also be pecking because they are bored. Entertain and distract them by adding fresh grass clippings to the brooder several times a day. Trimming the beak of an aggressive chick is an option if these other remedies fail (see page 163).

Birds that have been pecked should be isolated until the wounds heal. Chicks will get aggressive at the site of blood and the pecking will intensify. Treat the injured chick with a topical disinfectant or antibacterial cream. Some creams available also include ingredients like cayenne that taste awful to the aggressors and deter continued pecking.

The First Few Weeks & Your Five-Minute Daily Routine

After the first three days you and your chicks will settle into an easy daily routine.

- Your chicks will need fresh water fortified with Quik Chik and chick starter feed sprinkled with baby grit every day. Most birds raised for egg production (as opposed to meat production) won't overeat, so you don't need to worry about overfeeding your chicks. Just keep a steady supply of water and feed available. You'll see your chicks starting to eat more as they grow larger.

- Observe your chicks daily to make sure the brooder is comfortable for them. Each week, as the chicks grow, you'll need to expand the brooder's size (see page 69) as you lower the temperature (at right) of the brooder. You'll also need to clean it, which is easy to do when you are making it larger. Bedding that needs to be cleaned more than once a week is one sign that your chicks are outgrowing their home.

- To keep the birds comfortable and minimize odors you will need to clean the brooder. A well set-up brooder lined with newspaper is easy to clean once a week or whenever it appears soiled. To clean the brooder, simply move your chicks to another safe, warm space, like a box beside the brooder. You'll also need to remove the chick feeder and waterer. Fold up the newspaper lining to gather and contain the soiled bedding. The bedding can be disposed of in your trash or added to a compost pile. It becomes good fertilizer. Line the brooder with new newspaper (and make it larger if necessary) and add an inch (2.5 cm) of new bedding. Then replace the waterer and feeder, check the temperature and return the chicks to their brooder.

- Between regular cleanings, watch for wet bedding around the waterers. Scoop out the wet bedding and add a little fresh bedding to keep the brooder dry. If the brooder is lightly soiled with chick droppings, you can add a new layer of bedding on top of the old between weekly cleanings.

BROODER TEMPERATURE

Each week, you'll need to raise the heat lamp to reduce the amount of heat in the brooder in order to maintain a comfortable temperature for your growing chicks. The first week, the brooder should be between 90°F-95°F (32°C-35°C). Reduce the temperature in the brooder by about 5°F (3°C) every week. After the fifth week, your chicks will likely have developed feathers, which will help them regulate their own heat. They should no longer need the additional heat from the heat lamp unless the weather in your area is particularly cold.

Week one: 90°F-95°F (32°C-35°C)

Week two: 85°F-90°F (29°C-32°C)

Week three: 80°F-85°F (26.6°C-29°C)

Week four: 75°F-80°F (23.8°C-26.6°C)

Week five: 70°F-75°F (21°C-23.8°C)

After week five: If your chicks have developed feathers, they won't need additional heat unless your area is particularly cold.

▲ Every morning and evening check that your chicks have plenty of water fortified with Quik Chik and feed sprinkled with grit.

▲ Observe your chicks for a moment:
Are they active and happy?

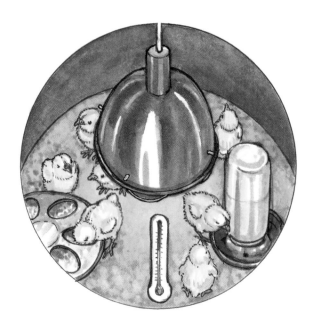

▲ Lower the brooder temperature per the schedule (see page 85).

▲ Clean the brooder quickly.

HINTS FROM THE HATCHERY

CURT MCCOSKEY

Years at Murray McMurray Hatchery: 37

Favorite breeds: Blue Andalusian and Blue Cochin

"I just enjoy watching the chickens and having them around. I raised a free-range flock, and it was fun to watch the birds interact with the other animals, the dogs, the cats, the kids. Chickens are cool. I like to think I still learn something about chickens every day."

GOOD HEALTH HABITS

It's important to take basic health precautions when handling your birds, for their sake and yours. Developing good sanitary habits is especially important if children will be playing with the chicks. The young chicks haven't yet developed a strong immune system and are very vulnerable to disease, and even chicks born in sanitary hatcheries can carry diseases. The incidence of serious contagions, like salmonella, among hatchery chicks is very low, but it's easy to reduce even limited risk with a few commonsense rules.

- Always wash your hands with antibacterial soap or use hand sanitizer before and after handling your chicks.
- Don't kiss or cuddle the chicks near your face as the mouth is a main point of disease transmission.
- Handle your chicks carefully. As newborns, they are fragile and even a short fall might injure them.
- If one of the chicks appears ill or is injured by pecking, isolate her in a warm, safe place with ample food and water until she heals.

CHICKEN TV

Your chicks will provide you with hours of entertainment. Watching their antics is so addictive that many backyard chicken farmers think of it as "Chicken TV" or "Chicken-vision." Newly hatched chicks scamper around the brooder and tussle with one another playfully like puppies, before collapsing in exhaustion. If you make the slightest noise, they'll awake suddenly and begin their antics again.

▲ Chicks in a brooder are like kids on a playground, running and jumping and tussling.
They are establishing a pecking order, which determines which chick will rule the roost.

Many backyard chicken farmers give their chicks names. Some chicks will even learn to come when they are called. As you bond with your flock and recognizable personalities emerge in individual chicks, your personal Chicken TV can take on all the drama of an afternoon soap opera.

What you're observing on your Chicken TV is your newly hatched chicks exploring their new world and finding their place in the pecking order. The commonly used term "pecking order" originally came from observations of the strict social hierarchy among chickens. The pecking order dictates which chicken gets to eat first, which one gets to sleep wherever she wants, and which one gets to peck and which one gets pecked. This is true even in a flock of two. It's a bit like life in middle school. Life in the flock might get a little rough and tumble as the pecking order is established, but once a chick emerges at the top of the hierarchy and the rest of the chicks find their place in the order, down to the last rung, a pecking order will help keep peace in the flock. Keep in mind, the pecking order does make it difficult to add new chickens to an established flock (see page 169).

You can help keep the flock happy by ensuring that the birds have plenty of space, which allows the lower-ranking chicks to avoid the higher ranking ones, and by providing enough waterer and feeder space to ensure the dominant chicks don't frighten away the others.

STRESS-FREE TRANSITION TO THE COOP

Two factors will help you decide when it's time to move your sweet chicks from their brooder to their outdoor coop—how big and boisterous they are and the outdoor temperature.

THE MURRAY MCMURRAY METHOD FIVE-MINUTE ROUTINE: THE FIRST FEW WEEKS

You only need to spend five minutes a day caring for your chicks, but chances are you'll want to spend a lot more time with the funny, endearing birds. The more time you spend interacting with the birds as chicks the friendlier and more sociable they will be throughout their lives.

THE MURRAY MCMURRAY METHOD: YOUR FIVE-MINUTE DAILY ROUTINE

Water
Fill the waterers with fresh water fortified with Quik Chik twice a day.

Feed
Fill the chick feeder with chick starter feed sprinkled with baby grit.

Observe
Do your chicks appear warm enough? Adjust the heat lamp accordingly.

Do they have enough space? If not, increase the brooder size.

Is the bedding wet, especially around the waterer? Scoop out the wet bedding and add additional bedding as needed.

THE MURRAY MCMURRAY METHOD: YOUR WEEKLY ROUTINE

Heat
Raise the heat lamp once a week to reduce the temperature in the brooder by 5°F (3°C).

Clean
Remove and replace the bedding in the brooder.

As your chicks reach four to six weeks, their newborn fuzz will be replaced with feathers, which help them better maintain their body temperature. Suddenly they will start to fly over the walls of their brooder. Once the weather is warm enough, the birds are ready to transition to the coop. If your birds haven't fully feathered (different breeds mature at different times) or the weather is still chilly, only move them to the coop if it has a supplemental heat source (see page 108).

Your goal is to make the transition as stress-free as possible for both you and the birds. Prepare the coop with food and water and warm it with the heat lamp so it is 65°F–70°F (18°C–21°C) if it's cold outside. If the coop is larger than the necessary 1 ½ to 2 square feet (.138 to .185 square meters) per standard bird, you should create a temporary wall or barrier of cardboard to confine the birds to one portion of the coop, close to the food and water, for a day or two until they feel comfortable in their new space. For the first several days, you can also keep the door to the run closed to give your birds time to adjust to their new home before introducing another new environment. When you do open the door to the run for the first time, don't be concerned if your birds don't run outside right away. It might take a couple more days before they start to explore. Keep the food and water in the coop while the birds are getting used to things so that they get in the habit of returning to the coop.

Once the birds start exploring both the coop and the run, and start roosting on the waterer, their food and water will become dirtier (from dust and bedding) move quickly. Clean the food and water as needed.

As always keep an eye on your chicks—now chickens—in their new home. Are they eating, drinking and exploring? Or has the stress of the move caused them to start pecking at each other? You have experience as a chicken farmer now and the same tricks you learned in the first weeks will help you know if you have a happy flock or an unhappy bird.

chapter 5

THE MURRAY MCMURRAY METHOD for RAISING CHICKENS in FIVE MINUTES a DAY

EVERYTHING YOU NEED TO KNOW FOR SUCCESSFUL BACKYARD CHICKEN FARMING

The key to raising happy, healthy chickens in just a few minutes a day is good preparation and a regular routine.

GETTING READY

This is what you've been waiting for, your own flock of chickens in your own backyard! This chapter teaches you all you need to do to prepare the coop for your fast-growing chicks and then how to care for them in just five minutes a day.

In the month or so since your chicks arrived you've watched the sweet hatchlings grow into young chickens, as their fluffy down was replaced with pretty feathers. You are already an experienced backyard chicken farmer, with a five-minute daily routine of caring for your chicks. As you transfer the birds to their coop, you'll start a new five-minute daily routine and will soon be enjoying both the company of your chickens and their delicious eggs.

Once you have set up an efficient chicken coop and run in your backyard with the chicken feed, water and other supplies nearby, you and your chickens will fall into an easy and fun daily routine. Visiting your chickens in the morning to feed and water them and collect their freshly laid eggs will be a treat, not a chore. Even cleaning the coop once a month will be a simple task.

THE CHICKEN SUPPLY CHECKLIST

These are the supplies you'll need prior to moving the chicks to your backyard. The items are further described in this chapter.

- Coop, sized to allow 1 ½ to 2 square feet (.138 to .185 square meters) of space per bird: $300-$2000, depending on size and amenities

- Run, 10 to 20 square feet (.93 to 1.86 square meters) for a flock of up to 12: About $200

- Nesting boxes (one nesting box for every five birds): About $16 to $50 each

- 1 perch with at least 8 inches (20.3 cm) of space per bird

- Bedding to cover the coop about 2 inches (5.1 cm) deep at each monthly cleaning

- Diatomaceous earth (see page 120): About $17

- Hose or bucket

- Rodent-proof feed storage such as a large outdoor trash can (25 to 45 gallons) with a tight-fitting lid: approximately $30 to $100

- Water heater, optional, about $50

- Light (use a red bulb if pecking is a problem) about $30

The following items are sufficient for a flock of up to 12 chickens:

- 1 five-gallon (3.785 liters) waterer: About $35

- 1 thirty-five-pound (15.88 kg) capacity feeder: About $30

- 1 fifty-pound (23 kg) bag of feed (enough for one to two weeks): About $45

- 1 five-pound (2.27 kg) bag of chicken grit for adults (will last a long time): About $10

- 1 five-pound (2.27 kg) bag of food-grade crushed oyster shells (enough for a few months): About $10

You'll also need:

- Egg basket

- Egg cartons

- Dust mask, for cleaning

- Dust broom

- Rake

- Wheelbarrow or bucket

SETTING UP THE MOST CONVENIENT CHICKEN COOP, NESTING BOXES AND RUN

The coop is your chickens' home; the attached run is their playground; the nesting boxes are where they will lay their eggs. Your chickens will spend most of their days in the run, eating, watering, scratching in the dirt, exploring and entertaining you with their antics. They will spend their nights in the coop, roosting and entering the nesting boxes in the early morning to lay their eggs. It is important to have a door to the coop that you can open in the morning and close in the evening to separate the coop from the run.

The coop, nesting boxes and run, which can be purchased separately or as a unit, must be designed with your chickens' health and safety in mind. That means choosing a coop and run that are large enough for your flock and are properly fortified against predators, with a door that closes the chickens into the coop at night. You will also need to install enough cozy nesting boxes for your flock.

The coop, nesting boxes and run should also be designed for your convenience. We recommend a raised coop, which allows for cleaning without stooping and helps with rodent infestation. The coop should be designed so the hinged roof or side wall lifts to provide access to the nesting box(es), allowing you to collect the eggs easily and clean the coop with ease. Lucky is the backyard farmer who has a run tall enough to stand in, but the chickens certainly don't need all that height, so runs with less height are fine if you are prepared to crouch at times.

The Ideal Coop Location

When selecting a location for your chicken coop and run, consider your chickens' needs first, but don't neglect your own convenience, or consideration for your neighbors, who may or may not find your chickens an awesome addition to the neighborhood. Although properly-cared for chickens aren't noisy or foul-smelling, your neighbors may prefer that you place your coop out of sight or away from property lines. Local regulations may offer some restrictions as well. Taking your neighbors' concerns into consideration may help relations, as will some fresh eggs once your hens start laying. On the other hand, your neighbors may love watching your chickens so you might want to place the coop somewhere convenient for them and other visitors to enjoy some "Chicken TV."

YOUR ULTIMATE COOP

Coop door: A door between the coop and the run so you can close your chickens in the coop at night and keep them safe.

Nesting boxes: Nesting boxes in which the chickens lay their eggs. It is most convenient when boxes open to the exterior to make egg collection easy.

Windows and artificial light: Hens need 15 to 16 hours of light each day to produce eggs. Windows allow natural light into the coop and reduce the need for artificial light.

Ventilation: Ventilation keeps the coop dry. A dry coop needs to be cleaned less often.

Hinged roof: A hinged roof or hinged sidewall makes monthly cleaning easier.

Waterer and feeder: Containers that hold water and feed for the chickens.

Coarse bedding: The bedding in the coop absorbs the chicken waste; in nesting boxes it provides a soft cushion for the hens and their eggs.

Pool: Your chickens will love bathing in diatomaceous earth; it also reduces parasites.

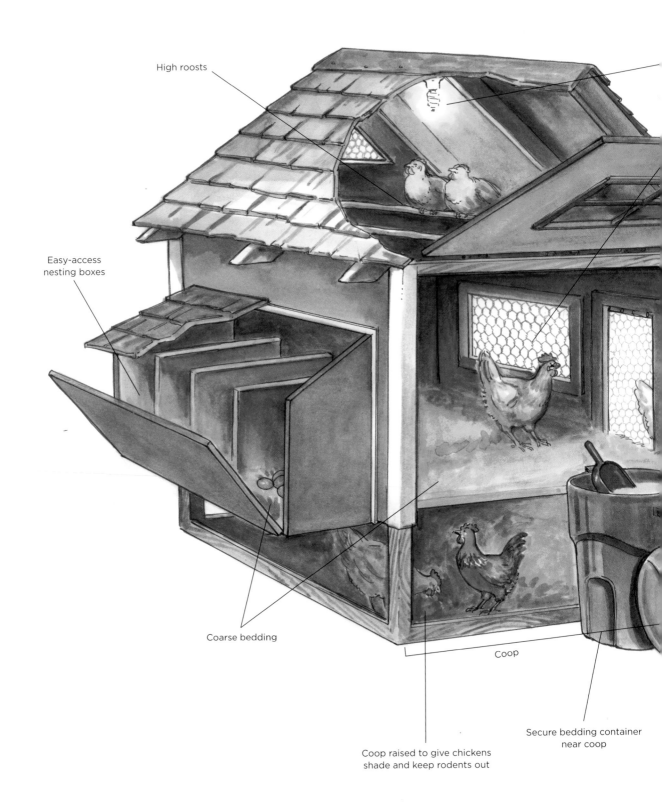

High roosts

Easy-access
nesting boxes

Coarse bedding

Coop

Coop raised to give chickens
shade and keep rodents out

Secure bedding container
near coop

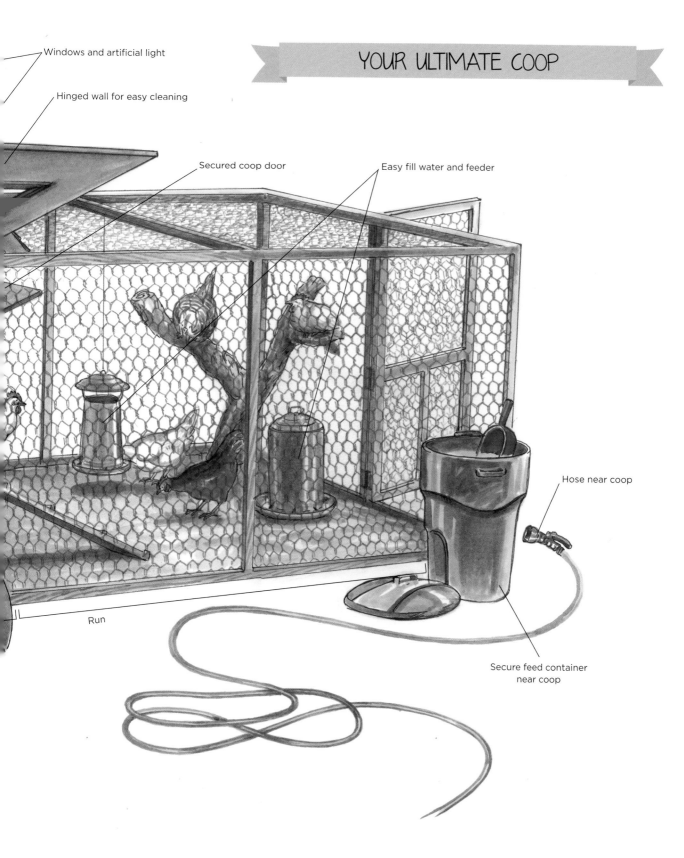

Windows and artificial light

Hinged wall for easy cleaning

Secured coop door

Easy fill water and feeder

Hose near coop

Run

Secure feed container
near coop

The coop provides your chickens with protection from both predators and the elements. When choosing a location, be sure that your chickens will have access to sunlight, for warming themselves on colder days, and shade for cooling off on warmer ones. You'll also want to choose a location that provides some shelter from winds. Your chickens will be better egg producers if they have a calm environment in and around their coop. Avoid any location with loud noises, lurking predators or a busy road.

For your convenience, consider placing the coop near your house. Easy access to your home's water for filling the chicken waterer and electricity for lighting and/or heating the coop will make your daily routine easier and quicker. You'll also want a location where you can store a supply of feed, grit, crushed oyster shells and bedding nearby to help speed up your daily routine.

A chicken tractor, one style of coop, favored by many backyard chicken farmers, eliminates the location question. A chicken tractor is a combination coop and run that takes on many different shapes. Every chicken tractor, regardless of the shape, is bottomless and designed to be moved on a regular basis, giving the chickens access to fresh grass and insects in the dirt, and fertilizing your yard with chicken manure. This type of coop is useful to backyard chicken farmers with a small flock of about six chickens (otherwise, the coop would be too large to move easily) and a sizeable yard with several good coop locations.

The Best Coop for Your Backyard

As long as your chickens' basic needs for shelter are met, there are as many suitable styles of backyard chicken coops as there are backyard chicken farmers. Your coop and run can be as simple as a plywood hutch with a nesting box made from a five-gallon plastic bucket with a door leading to a wire-enclosed run. Or it can be a veritable chicken mansion, outfitted to look like a classic barn, a log cabin or a near-replica of your own house.

Although some coops with wire flooring are available, it's not recommended to raise chickens on wire as it can injure their feet. You also want to avoid treated woods or toxic paints and stains which can give off unhealthy gases. No matter their exterior design, all chicken coops have the same basic requirements.

Chicken Coop Essentials

SPACE

Providing enough space for your flock inside the coop is essential. Plan on 1 ½ to 2 square feet (.138 to .185 square meters) per bird in the coop. Too little space can lead to pecking among the flock and will need more frequent cleaning. Too much space can also be a concern in colder climates, since a flock living in a well-sized and draft-free coop can often maintain a comfortable coop temperature through body heat.

- 6 to 8 square feet (.58 to .74 square meters) for a flock of four
- 9 to 12 square feet (.84 to 1.11 square meters) for a flock of six
- 18 to 24 square feet (1.67 to 2.23 square meters) for a flock of twelve
- 30 to 40 square feet (2.79 to 3.72 square meters) for a flock of twenty

▲ A chicken coop must provide shelter and protection for your flock, but once those basic needs are met, anything goes. Some backyard chicken farmers choose simple, practical coops (like the chicken tractor, top left); some create elaborate houses.

LIGHT

Your hens require 15 to 16 hours of light each day to encourage egg production. A coop with windows allows daylight to naturally regulate their laying cycles. If the windows are open, you should cover them with wire to discourage pests and predators. If you want to encourage your flock to continue laying when the days begin to shorten, you'll need artificial lighting in the coop (see page 134).

VENTILATION

Ventilation is essential for preventing a dusty, smelly coop. A poorly ventilated coop isn't just unpleasant for you as the backyard chicken farmer; it's also unhealthy for your flock. The buildup of ammonia from their manure can cause eye irritation and discourage egg laying. Some coops have vents for cross ventilation, a feature you might consider as long as the vents are secured to deter rodents from entering the coop.

INSULATION

While ventilation is important, it's equally important to have a draft-free coop, especially in cold-weather locations. Look for a solidly-constructed coop. It doesn't need insulation like a house, it just needs to be sealed so most of it is draft-free. In some extreme locations, supplemental heat might be necessary but in most climates, even where the mercury can dip below 10 degrees, your chickens will do just fine in a well-built coop. If you do need supplemental heat for extreme weather, use a safe, tip-proof electric or propane heater or heat lamp strongly secured and located away from anything flammable. Chickens, like small birds in the wild, puff out their feathers and huddle together to stay warm.

DOOR

A closed door is your flocks' last line of defense against predators that might slip into the run. A coop door should be opened in the morning, giving the flock the opportunity to wander between the coop and the run throughout the day. It should be closed in the evening when the chickens have returned to the coop for protection.

NESTING BOXES

You want to encourage your hens to lay their eggs in nesting boxes. These boxes, which are usually about 14 inches (35.6 cm) high and wide, should be small, dark and safe places for your chickens to lay their eggs. Eggs laid in a nesting box, which is usually installed about a foot (30.5 cm) off the ground, will typically be cleaner than those laid on the floor of the coop. There is also less danger of eggs breaking when they are laid in the nesting boxes.

If your nesting boxes have a hinged cover, collecting eggs will be easier. Plan for at least one nesting box per five birds. If you have room for two, even if you have a smaller flock, you'll still have a spare if you end up with a broody hen (see page 133). You do not need to install nesting boxes in your coop until your flock is about 18 to 24 weeks old, which is laying age, depending on the breed.

PERCHES

Depending on the breed, your chickens may appreciate a raised place to roost. It gives them a feeling of security when they are sleeping and a place to escape when they feel threatened. Some coops have built-in perches and some nesting boxes are equipped with them. Otherwise, they can be added to the coop.

EASY ACCESS

A hinged roof or hinged sidewall gives the backyard chicken farmer convenient access to the coop for cleaning and gathering the eggs.

TIPS FOR PROTECTING YOUR CHICKENS FROM PESTS AND PREDATORS

The coop and run should be designed to protect your chickens from common pests and predators in your region. Almost any animal can be a pest or predator, even your own dog. Pest and predators can come from any direction and frighten the hens, which inhibits egg production. Small rodents, which sometimes carry disease, can burrow under fencing or enter through windows and vents. Hawks can swoop down from above. Coyotes, wolves, and dogs can attack free-range hens or try to get through the wire run.

- A well-secured, properly sized, clean, raised coop will protect your flock day and night.

- A run with strong, tightly woven 12- or 16-gauge wire walls will provide your flock the necessary security.

- Rodent-proof storage for feed will discourage would-be pests and predators.

- When you visit the coop, always check for signs of intruders. Even small holes can let pests and predators slip in. Although prevention is best, place rodent traps quickly at the first signs of their presence so they don't have a chance to establish themselves.

- Close the coop door each evening when many predators are on the prowl.

- Dogs typically like to chase chickens, and a dog can severely injure or kill a chicken even when it is just playing. They may also try to get into the coop or run to steal the chickens' food. Sometimes dogs will follow the chickens from outside the run as the chickens wander about inside. Most dogs can be trained to stay away from the chickens, but it can be a hard habit to break if the dog is already used to chasing them (see page 79).

▲ There are many predators lurking in your backyard. Even your pet dog can be a danger to the flock if not properly trained. Remember to secure your coop to help keep other predators (including other dogs) away.

Setting Up the No-fuss Feed System

Chickens aren't picky eaters. In the wild, a flock would scratch out their diet in the fields, eating seeds, fruits, insects, even small mammals. In your coop, however, your chickens rely on you to provide the nutrition they need through chicken feed, grit, crushed oyster shells and the occasional kitchen scraps. In return, well-nourished hens will provide an abundance of delicious eggs for you.

Your chickens eat small meals throughout the day and don't eat in darkness. Most backyard chicken farmers utilize a chicken feeder that continually dispenses feed as the flock eats to ensure that the chickens always have access to dry and pest-free feed. These feeders also minimize waste because they prevent the chickens from playing in the feed. The best location for the feeder is inside the coop, where it is less likely to attract predators and pests and is protected from rain and mold that can develop with moisture.

It's a cinch to refill the feeder each morning when you open the door to the run and collect your eggs, especially if you store the feed (with a scoop) nearby in a rodent-proof container. In addition to chicken feed, you'll want to store grit and crushed oyster shells nearby.

FEED

Chicken feed is most often a mix of corn and soymeal, however the protein content varies among feeds. When your chicks were in the brooder, they ate chick starter rations with an 18 to 20% protein level. When they move to the coop at four or six weeks old, you'll switch them to a grower ration with a 14 to 16% protein level. At fourteen to sixteen weeks, about two to four weeks before they begin laying eggs, replace the grower rations with layer rations, which have a 16 to 18% protein level. Chicken feed is available in several forms, as pellets, crumbles or mash, which is terminology that describes its consistency. Many backyard chicken farmers find that pellets for mature chickens make for the cleanest coop, the least waste and less dust. When choosing a feed, remember that when you eat their eggs, you're eating what your chickens ate. You might want to consider organic rations if organic farming is important to you and the rations are available. Be aware of any medications in the feed and refer to the label for any restrictions on consuming the eggs of chickens eating medicated feed.

In buying feed, plan for about 2 to 4 pounds (.9 to 1.8 kg) of grower or layer rations per standard chicken per week. This is between ¼ and ½ pound (.11 to .22 kg) per day for each chicken, although the amount does vary some with the size of the breed. Bantams only need about ¼ pound (.11 kg) each week. You can buy feed in bulk to save time and money, but don't let your feed expire or become moldy.

Be aware of any drastic changes in the eating habits of your chickens, although some change is normal. For instance, your flock will eat more in the winter, when they are expending more energy to stay warm and when snacks, such as worms, grasshoppers or other creatures in the grass and dirt of the run, are less available.

GRIT

Grit helps chickens grind up and digest their food. It is nothing more than finely ground stone that collects in the chicken's digestive system to pulverize denser and more fibrous meals. In the wild, these stones can come from the soil, but most backyard chickens don't have enough access to natural grit, so you should give them processed grit. The finely ground "chick grit" is appropriate for chicks in the brooder; a slightly coarser chicken grit for adults is appropriate for mature chickens in the coop. Grit can be offered to the flock as "free choice" in a bowl separate from the food that the birds can visit when they need the digestive assistance, or it can be mixed in with the feed. If you mix grit with the feed, use a light hand. A cup (250 ml) of grit, well-distributed, is enough for a 50-pound (22.7 kg) bag of feed. If your birds are eating around the grit and some remains in the feeder when the food is gone, you are adding too much.

CRUSHED OYSTER SHELLS

Feed-grade crushed oyster shells are a calcium supplement for your flock that strengthens eggshells. Most feed already has the right amount of calcium but many chicken farmers supplement their feed with crushed oyster shells to keep eggs and egg production healthy. Crushed oyster shells are most often offered by free choice, in a separate bowl or feeder, but they can be added to the feed. Add about 10 to 12 cups (1 to 1.5 kg) of crushed oyster shells per 50-pound (22.7 kg) bag of feed or half that for a 25-pound (11.3 kg) bag of feed. Again, your birds will eat around the oyster shells if they don't need the calcium.

WHAT ELSE CAN YOU FEED YOUR CHICKENS?

Grower or layer rations with the appropriate protein level, grit and crushed oyster shells are necessary staples of your flock's diet, but you can also feed your chickens many other things. Toss some table scraps into their run when you visit the flock and your chickens will be even more eager to see you each day. Chickens will also eat old fruit and vegetables but don't give them rotten or moldy ones.

Most chickens love "scratch," a chicken treat of corn, oats and seeds. You can give them up to ½ cup (125 g) of scratch a day for every six chickens in your flock. You can also feed your flock from your table, just keep in mind that supplementing your chickens' diet, can affect the quality of the eggs they produce. Choose good, nutritious foods; avoid any high fat, high sugar or highly processed foods. Dark, leafy green vegetables are particularly good for your flock, especially if they have limited access to greenery in their run.

You should avoid feeding your chickens anything with strong flavors, like onions and garlic, which can change the taste of the eggs. You should also avoid feeding them raw potato peels, dried beans, avocado skins and pits, citrus and anything extremely salty. These can all be toxic to your flock, and it goes without saying that you shouldn't feed your chickens alcohol or caffeine.

You should also avoid feeding your chickens' raw eggs, because you want to do everything you can to discourage the chickens from eating the eggs in the coop. Hard-boiled and peeled eggs or scrambled eggs are fine. Although cooked meats are a suitable treat, most backyard chicken farmers avoid feeding cooked chicken to their chickens, just on principle.

Setting up the Quickest Watering System

An average chicken will drink one to two cups (250 to 500 ml) of water a day, even more in the warm summer months, and laying hens consume even more water since eggs are primarily water. Your job as a backyard chicken farmer is to provide your flock with a constant source of clean water. Hens deprived of water for 24 hours often stop laying eggs and any chicken deprived of water for longer than a day can die of dehydration, so it's important to stay on top of the water supply.

▲ Chickens in the coop need only a few minutes' attention each day and a steady supply of food and water.

It's easy to meet your chickens' water needs with multiple waterers, filled once a day. Even the smallest flock should have two waterers available, one in the coop and one in the run, to encourage consumption.

There are many different types of chicken waterers available. The simplest are bell-shaped, with water running from a large drum into a narrow trough as the chickens drink. More elaborate versions automatically pump water from a well. Simple or elaborate, all good waterers are designed to store enough water for your flock's daily needs and to keep the water clean of bedding or chicken droppings. A sturdy waterer that won't collapse or tip when your chickens roost on it is another consideration.

If your coop is located near a water source, you can simply use a hose to fill the waterers each morning, just remember to empty any dirty water from the waterer first. A water fixture fitted with a splitter, so one hose can be dedicated to the coop, is very convenient, as is a hose with a shutoff valve at the end. And, while a chicken waterer is very helpful, you can always use a 10-or 12-quart (9.5 to 11.4 liters) rubber bucket and fill it from your sink or hose. Don't get a larger bucket because it will be too heavy to carry easily.

Your chickens might be picky about the temperature of their water. They don't like water too cold (and it's useless to them frozen!) and they don't like it too warm. In the summer months, fill the waterers with cool water and place them out of direct sunlight. In the winter months, fill the waterers with warm water and place in the sunlight or near supplemental heat.

If the waterers take on an unpleasant smell or show signs of bacteria growth, clean them thoroughly with diluted bleach.

WINTER WATERING THE EASY WAY

If you live in a cold climate you will need a different winter watering strategy. You have a couple of good options. If you have electricity in the coop and run or can reach an extension cord to the coop, you can buy a heater for a tin waterer, which will keep the water from freezing even when the temperature drops to about 10°F (-12°C). You can back up this system when it gets really cold by putting warm water in a 10-or 12-quart (9.5 to 11.4 liters) rubber bucket (you'll need two) and replacing them each day. Bring the frozen bucket in, let it thaw then dump the big ice cube before refilling.

Some chicken farmers in cold climates use three or four 10-or 12-quart (9.5 to 11.4 liters) buckets all the time so they don't need power, don't need to hassle with changing the waters and can fill the bucket inside where it's warm. To rotate buckets, keep one bucket in the run and one in the coop with both just off the ground so the chickens can't knock them over. Fill two buckets with warm water in the morning and replace the frozen ones. When it warms up, you won't have to replace the water every day, just a couple of times a week.

Setting up For Efficient Maintenance

The key to keeping your daily chicken routine to five minutes or less is to store the basic maintenance equipment near the coop. Having extra bedding, a bedding scoop, a rake, a wheelbarrow and some coop cleaning supplies as well as feed nearby makes the relatively quick process of cleaning and maintaining the chicken coop even easier.

You'll need to clean the coop whenever it looks soiled or begins to smell, which is unlikely to be more than once a month. But you should add some bedding to the nesting boxes every day when you collect the eggs. The cleaner the nesting boxes, the cleaner the eggs. Also, the bedding will absorb any broken eggs and keep your chickens from eating them. Even if you have limited space, keep a small amount of bedding and a scoop near the coop for this purpose.

Although your regular daily visit to the chicken coop won't be a messy one, it's good practice to wear "coop clothes" when interacting with your chickens. This helps prevent you from carrying germs or bacteria from the house to the coop or vice versa. Wearing a pair of work gloves and washing your hands before and after tending to the flock is sufficient for most daily chores. A work shirt or jacket and a pair of shoes that you wear only in the coop are recommended when you are cleaning or doing other maintenance inside the coop.

STEP-BY-STEP: CARING FOR YOUR CHICKENS

Both you and your chickens will appreciate a daily routine, which culminates in collecting (and probably eating) fresh eggs. Your chickens will come to know you, expect you and even follow you around in the run.

Your Chickens' Daily Routine

Your chickens will become predictable, but no less entertaining for it.

During the daylight hours, they will be active, eating little meals, drinking sips of water, scratching in the dirt, chucking and clucking and interacting with each other and you. They will wander from the run to the coop, seeking out sun or shade, or protection from rain.

During the day, they will also like to dust bathe. Fill a small baby pool with diatomaceous earth for your chickens to play in and clean themselves with the light, abrasive dirt (actually the fossilized remains of a type of algae). They will love it! Watching your chickens play in diatomaceous earth is fun, but the dust bath also helps prevent mites and parasites.

As night approaches, the chickens will return to the coop like clockwork and when it's dark, they will fall into a deep slumber. If your birds' laying cycles are well managed, they will most likely lay eggs in the nesting boxes in the early morning, where eggs will be waiting for you when you arrive in the morning.

Your Five-Minute Daily Routine

The traditional image of a farmer is someone who wakes with the dawn, ready to tend to the livestock and fields. The backyard chicken farmer doesn't have to be quite so prompt. More important than the early wake-up call is consistency. If you maintain a consistent routine, your birds will, too, laying eggs predictably in the early-morning hours.

Every morning you'll need to release the chickens from the coop, refill their water and food, replenish the grit and crushed oyster shells as needed, collect and store the eggs, tidy up the nesting boxes and observe your chickens and the coop. The only variation to this routine is in the winter when you might need your winter watering strategy.

- If your water source is near the coop, you can wash your hands and head right out to visit the flock with a basket for egg collecting and any table scraps you have for the flock. If you don't have a water source near the coop, fill your watering bucket and take it with you.

- Your chickens will probably be excited to see you when you open the coop door and toss any treats you brought into the run. Empty any dirty water from the waterers and then fill them with the water from your bucket or from the nearby water source. Fill the feeders with the chicken feed stored in the nearby, rodent-proof feed container. Check the grit and crushed oyster shell supply, if you offer free choice, and add some as needed.

▲ It is funny to watch a chicken "dust bathe" in diatomaceous earth. Bonus: Chickens love it, too, and it can reduce pests and parasites in the flock.

- By now your chickens will most likely be in the run, nibbling on their treats and scratching about. You can head to the nesting boxes and collect the eggs to fill your basket. Add a fresh scoop of bedding to each nesting box from a nearby container.

- Collect and throw away any eggs fouled with chicken poop to prevent the possible spread of disease; it is okay to eat an egg that has mud on it as long as you wash it well.

- Before you head back indoors with your fresh eggs (and one empty water bucket), look around the coop. Do you see any signs of predators or pests? Is the bedding dry or will the coop need a cleaning soon? Then watch your flock for a moment. Are they active and healthy? Are they eating and drinking? Watching your birds is one of the best parts of backyard chicken farming and an important way for you to know if your flock has everything it needs.

- If you have time, spend it interacting with your chickens. The more you do, the more likely your birds are to be friendly and affectionate with you and with visitors you bring to the coop. You should feel comfortable picking up your birds. The easiest way to lift a chicken is with two hands, one on the bird's back and the other around the bird's legs. Once you've picked up the bird, you can cradle the bird in the crook of your arm, still grasping the legs. One funny thing you'll notice about chickens is that because their eyes operate differently than humans' eyes, when you move the chicken's body from side to side, it will extend its neck to keep its head in a steady position.

- When you return to the house, wash your hands again and examine, clean and store the fresh eggs.

- In the evening you'll need to return to the coop to close the coop door once your flock is inside for the night. If you are using a light to extend the laying season (see page 134), turn it on. And since you're there anyway, check for any eggs you might have missed.

TIMED LIGHT

If consistency isn't always a possibility, you can invest in an automatic coop door and timed light. This Murray McMurray Hatchery invention makes life even easier for the backyard chicken farmer, keeping your flock to a routine, even when you sleep a little late. The automatic door uses a light sensor to open at sunrise and close at sunset, while a thermometer prevents the door from opening if the temperature is below 20°F (-6°C). Eight hours after sunset a timer turns on the artificial light, encouraging early-morning egg production.

▲ There is nothing more satisfying than collecting and sharing the delicious eggs from your backyard flock.

▲ Each morning, release your chickens from their coop.

▲ Fill the waterers with fresh water.

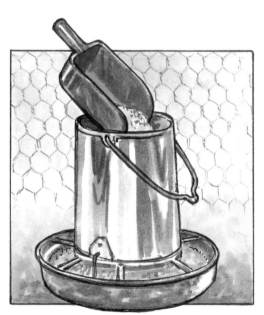

▲ Fill the feeders with the appropriate feed for your birds. Replenish oyster shells and grit, as needed, if you are offering it in separate containers.

▲ Collect the eggs and add a small scoop of bedding to each nest box.

▲ Observe your chickens and their home: Do they seem healthy? Is the coop secure?

▲ Each evening, the chickens will return to their coop. Shut the door behind them.

THE MURRAY MCMURRAY METHOD OF BACKYARD CHICKEN FARMING: A QUICK REFERENCE CHART

YOUR FIVE-MINUTE DAILY ROUTINE

Release

Open the door to the chicken coop to allow the chickens to wander from the coop to the run. Toss any treats you might have for the flock, such as scratch or table scraps, into the run to encourage them to exit the coop and make your chores easier.

Water

Fill the waterers with fresh water, after checking to make sure they are clean and, in the winter, unfrozen. Remember that your chickens will need more water in the summer and when they are laying.

Feed

Fill the feeders with the appropriate feed for your birds (see page 113). Replenish grit and crushed oyster shells as needed.

Collect

Once your flock begins to lay eggs, collect the eggs every day. As you do, add a small scoop of bedding to each nesting box. When you finish your chores in the coop, examine, clean and store the day's eggs.

Observe

Do your chickens appear healthy and active? Is the coop secure? Does some water and feed remain or are the waterer and feeder empty, a sign you need to increase the supply?

Secure

Return to the coop at sunset to close the coop door after your flock has returned. You can also check for additional eggs.

SHOULD YOUR FLOCK FREE-RANGE?

You don't have to confine your chickens to the coop and run. You can also raise them as free-range birds, releasing them from the coop and run (if you have one) during the day. There are benefits to this practice. Free-range birds are less likely to become bored and begin pecking each other. They will also have access to a more varied diet and eat less commercial feed as a result. Chickens are naturally homebodies and won't typically stray too far from the coop unless frightened by a predator. They instinctively return to the coop at dusk.

One of the drawbacks to allowing your chickens to free-range is predators. They are everywhere and a free-ranging flock is more susceptible than one confined to the coop and run. Your neighbors may also object to the same things you may love about free-ranging, that your chickens are underfoot or roosting in trees and on fence posts. Free-range chickens will fertilize the grass and control pests, but they can decimate lawns in the area where they spend the most time, and no one will be happy if the chickens get into the garden and eat all the lettuce.

It's fun to allow your flock to have free range, even if it's occasional. You might have to show them back into the coop the first two or three times, which will involve some chasing down of the chickens, but they will soon come back on their own. If you need to catch your chickens, bring a helper and a long stick. Use the stick to herd the chickens into the grasp of your helper.

▶ Your backyard will really feel like a farm if you allow your chickens to roam freely. Free-ranging chickens will naturally roost in the lower branches of your trees during the day and return to the coop at dusk.

▲ When you first let the chickens free range, they aren't used to finding and going back into the coop at dusk so you might have to catch a few of them or herd them into the run or coop once or twice. Some of your hens might be hard to catch. A long stick or broom handle can help. Hold the stick out to your side low to the ground and the chickens usually won't run under it. Then you can chase the chicken into a friend's legs to catch it or into the run and coop. If you can't catch one or two and your neighborhood seems predator free, leave them out for the night. They will hang around the coop and join the others in the morning. In less than a week and usually a couple of nights, the chickens figure out how to get back to the coop on their own.

ALL ABOUT EGGS

For most backyard chicken farmers, the fresh eggs are the real reward; fresh eggs that are a world away in flavor and texture from the supermarket variety. Once you taste them, you'll never want to go back to store-bought eggs again.

If you take care of your flock, they will produce an abundance of delicious eggs for you. A Pearl-White Leghorn, one of the most prolific layers, can produce a large egg almost every day for the majority of the year. That can mean more than 20 dozen eggs a year from just one bird.

You do not need a rooster to harvest eggs (and roosters won't lay eggs)! You need a rooster only if you want fertilized eggs to hatch and grow your flock. Hens will lay unfertilized eggs without a rooster present. You can eat both fertilized and unfertilized eggs. Most eggs you purchase at the supermarket are unfertilized.

▲ A well-designed coop makes it easy to collect your flock's eggs each morning. The promise of a delicious breakfast makes the "chore" everyone's favorite.

The First Eggs

Your hens will start laying eggs at about 18 to 24 weeks old. Each hen's first egg or two might be small, misshapen or soft. These are signs of a young hen, and after those first few eggs, you'll get consistently-shaped and firm eggs from your flock. If you were using medicated feed, don't eat the first soft eggs. An occasional odd egg from an older hen isn't a problem. If a hen is consistently laying a soft, misshapen or otherwise atypical egg, the hen might be ill. Try adding some crushed oyster shells and grit to her food and make sure you are providing her with enough water and feed. A backyard flock can lay eggs for many years, although production will decrease as hens get older.

Your hens will naturally lay their eggs in the nesting boxes you've installed in the coop. The small, dark spaces are attractive to the hen and once one hen starts using them the others will follow, as hens instinctively lay their eggs where others in the flock do. If you're finding eggs throughout the coop, or even in the run, you can purchase mock eggs or use golf balls to fill the nesting boxes with pretend "eggs." These pretend eggs should trick the hens into using the nesting boxes, which means cleaner eggs and more convenient egg collection.

Hens tend to lay their eggs in the early morning, entering the nesting box only to lay and then exiting. Of course, hens do lay eggs to reproduce and sometimes their mothering instincts kick in even though the eggs are unfertilized. If you open the door to a nesting box and find one of your hens sitting on her egg, she has gone "broody." A broody hen will sit on the eggs to warm them in preparation for the birth of chicks. A broody hen isn't sick, but she will stop laying and she will monopolize a nesting box. Some farmers have methods to stop the broodiness (see page 165) and others just let it pass.

Encouraging Egg Production

Happy, healthy hens are good egg producers. Beyond basic care, there are a few things you can do to encourage regular egg production.

LIGHTING

Hens naturally lay eggs more regularly in the warmer months. The length of the days and the strength of the sunlight encourage the production of the hormones necessary for the egg-laying process. You can fool your hens to keep them producing in cooler months by consistently adding artificial light to your backyard coop for 15 to 16 consecutive hours a day. A timer for the lights will keep the hens in a regular egg-laying routine and help keep the coop warm. You can turn it on at dusk and turn it off before you go to bed, or you can turn it on in the morning to heat the coop.

ROUTINE

Your hens will develop a laying routine. All you have to do is avoid disturbing it. If your hens are in the nesting box laying an egg (usually in the early morning), don't choose that time to clean the coop or invite visitors to meet your flock.

CALM

Avoid anything that will stress your egg-laying hens. Making sure your chickens are safe and well cared for will keep them calm and laying eggs regularly, but this is just common practice for the backyard chicken farmer.

Collecting the Eggs

Egg collection is a rewarding chore, one that even children can be enticed to do with the promise of a farm-fresh breakfast. You should collect the eggs from your coop at least once a day. If you leave an egg in the nesting box it might become dirty or cracked. In the winter it might freeze. And, worst of all, you may find that an egg was crushed and the hens are eating the yolk. You don't want your hens to discover that the egg yolk is delicious. It's hard to break an egg-eating hen of the bad habit and you'll almost certainly lose more eggs (see page 164).

Use a dedicated egg basket or egg cartons to collect the eggs from the nesting boxes each morning. Occasionally you'll find an egg outside of the nesting box. It's best to discard the egg if you don't know how long it has been there. Clean the eggs before storing them (page 136), but discard any egg that is especially soiled. Once you have checked all the nesting boxes and finished your other chores, bring the egg basket into the house to examine and clean the eggs. Check each egg carefully for any cracks. Cracked eggs can harbor bacteria and should be discarded, as should any that smell bad.

All your remaining eggs—even those that look clean—should be washed. Egg shells are porous, so it's important to clean the eggs in such a way that bacteria isn't drawn into the shell. Wash each good egg under warm running water. The water should be about 20 degrees Farenheight warmer than the egg. Rinse all the sides of the egg, not scrubbing hard, which might damage the shell, and dry it thoroughly before storing.

Commercial egg cartons are well-designed to keep eggs fresh and prevent them from absorbing other food odors through their porous shells. You can purchase egg cartons or collect them from friends with the promise of a fresh dozen. There is no need to sort the eggs by size as they are in a grocery store, but if you have different breeds laying distinctly different-size eggs, you might want to sort those. Consistently sized eggs aren't important for omelets but are essential in baking.

There is some debate over egg storage. In the United States, eggs are typically stored in the refrigerator. In other countries, particularly in Europe and South America, they are stored on the counter. Either way, cartons should be labeled with the date. Your eggs will last up to three months in the refrigerator. Rotate your egg stock so that none of your eggs get old before they are eaten. Slightly older eggs are better for boiling. Extremely fresh eggs can be tough to peel.

You can test the freshness of an uncracked, clean egg by submerging it in a bowl of water. A fresh egg will sink to the bottom of the bowl. An older egg will sink only partially, and the wider, rounded end will point upwards because some of the egg's contents have evaporated through its porous shell. A rotten egg will float.

If your flock is producing too many eggs for you and your family to consume, rejoice. Sharing or selling fresh eggs will make you friends. There are few people who won't appreciate the bright orange yolk and rich flavor of a freshly laid egg.

It's important to note that you only want to collect and eat eggs from a healthy flock. If your flock is ill or taking medication or eating medicated feed, follow the instructions on the packaging. It may instruct you to discard the collected eggs until the flock is healthy.

Managing the Molt

Molting is a chicken's natural process of losing and replacing feathers over approximately a two-month period. During this time hens stop laying eggs, or lay eggs sporadically, as their energy goes into feather production. Year-old pullets typically don't molt. Otherwise, chickens molt once a year, usually in the fall, when days begin to grow shorter. If you use artificial light in the coop to encourage egg production, you may also delay the molt. Keeping your flock well fed, watered and stress-free should prevent the molt from starting prematurely. All the birds in your flock won't necessarily molt at the same time, and the molt won't always be for the same duration. Healthy, productive hens that are fed higher protein rations during the molt can complete the process as quickly as four weeks.

Once your hens have their beautiful new feathers, they will return to laying, but their egg production may decrease with each molt.

THE QUICKEST COOP CLEAN UP

With the right equipment, which includes some old work clothes, a dust mask, a long-handled shovel, a dust brush and a wheelbarrow, cleaning your coop isn't the arduous task that many first-time backyard chicken farmers imagine. Plus, the coop does not usually need to be cleaned as often as you fear. Keep a set of dedicated cleaning tools that you use only to clean the coop so as not to carry dirt or disease into your house. Wear your old work clothes with a dust mask to prevent lung irritation.

If your coop is well ventilated and large enough for your flock, you might only need to clean it once a month, especially with some daily basic maintenance. Remember to add bedding to the nesting boxes to prevent dirty eggs. And be sure to fix a leaky roof or waterer to lengthen the period of time between full coop cleanings.

▲ Collect the equipment for easy coop cleaning: work clothes, a dust mask, a shovel or rake, dust brush and wheelbarrow.

▲ Empty all the bedding from the coop into the wheelbarrow.

▲ Use the dust brush to remove the bedding from the nesting boxes and harder-to-reach corners of the coop.

▲ Replace the soiled bedding with two to three inches of fresh bedding.

▲ Compost the soiled bedding. It will make great fertilizer.

Your coop needs to be cleaned when the bedding becomes damp or begins to smell of ammonia. Begin by closing the chickens in the run and removing the feeder and waterer. This is a good time to give those a thorough washing, too, but be sure the feeder is completely dry before refilling it so you don't start mold in the feed.

Using a shovel or rake, as needed, empty all the bedding from the coop into a bucket or, more conveniently, a wheelbarrow. A dust brush will help you get the bedding from the nesting boxes and the corners of the coop. Clean thoroughly, the better job you do, the longer it will be before you have to do it again.

Don't use a disinfectant in the coop unless you've had problems with disease. In fact, most backyard farmers don't use water to clean the coop. After all, dampness was what caused you to have to clean the coop in the first place. If you do use water, be sure the coop is completely dry before adding more bedding.

Once all of the soiled bedding is removed and you have dusted the coop, add two to three inches (5.1 to 7.6 cm) of fresh bedding to the floor and nesting boxes, return the waterer and feeder and let your chickens back into their home.

The only thing left to do is dispose of the soiled bedding. If you have the space, you can compost the bedding. After it has aged it's good fertilizer for flowers and trees. Putting the unmellowed bedding and manure on plants will burn them. Soiled bedding can also be buried or, in some communities, bagged and disposed of through regular trash pick up.

HINTS FROM THE HATCHERY

KENT BAHRENFUSS

Years at Murray McMurray Hatchery: 33 years

Favorite breeds: Salmon Faverolles and Blue Andalusian

"If you're going to raise livestock, chickens are something that don't require a lot of money. They don't require a lot of space and they don't require a lot of time, but you get a reward almost every day when you collect the eggs.

"The secret to raising chickens isn't really a secret. The cleaner you keep the coop, the healthier the birds are going to be. If you let things go in the coop-if the bedding is wet and soiled-the birds' health will suffer. But if you give them just a few minutes' attention each day and keep things clean, the birds are going to perform well for you."

chapter 6

MEET the BIRDS

CHOOSE FROM THE HUNDREDS OF CHICKEN BREEDS

Remember when you were choosing chickens for your backyard flock and you made a list of the characteristics that are important to you? There's a breed out there for everyone; the Murray McMurray Hatchery's online chick selector lists 18 variables, from egg color and size, to skin color and comb style. Here's a guide to the perks and quirks of the birds mentioned in this book, as well as some others to consider

Arucana/Americana

Araucana/Americana

This breed is a mix of Americana and Araucana chickens. The Araucana, which is an unusual chicken discovered in Chile, is crossbred to prevent a genetic flaw that can kill chicks. The Araucana typically produces a blue egg, but after crossbreeding the Araucana/Americana produces an Easter basket of green and blue eggs, with some hens even laying pink or yellow eggs. The mixed breed also produces unique chickens with small pea combs, a wide variety of colors and color patterns and a long laying season. They are typically more aloof than friendlier breeds, but birds, like people, are all different.

Size: Standard hen: 4 pounds (1.8 kg)

Eggs: Tinted

Millie Fleur Rooster

Belgian Bearded D'Uccle

A bantam-only breed that's known to be calm and friendly, the Bearded d'Uccle (and the closely related Booted Bantam, which doesn't have the full beard of the d'Uccle) is a striking bird with a low-set body, wide tail, white-tipped feathers and vulture hocks, or stiff feathers sticking out from the legs. The reddish Mille Fleur version is a favorite for backyard chicken farmers and early Dutch artists, who included the "Millies" in their paintings.

Size: Bantam hen: A little more than 1 ½ pounds (680 g)

Eggs: White

Blue Andalusian

Blue Andalusian

Originally from the Andalusia region of Spain, Blue Andalusian chickens have white skin, a medium single comb and—their defining characteristic—slate blue feathers. However, because the gene for blue feathers isn't dominant, only 50% of Blue Andalusian chicks will grow blue feathers; the others will be black, white or a combination. Blue Andalusians can be good free-range birds and are talkative and friendly if they are handled often.

Size: Standard hen: 5 ½ pounds (2.5 kg); Bantam hen: 1 ½ pounds (680 g)

Eggs: White

Silver-Laced Cochin

Cochin

The Cochin breed arrived from China in the mid-1800s. Known as friendly but poor layers (but good setters, if you want to hatch your eggs), Cochins are prized for their abundance of fluffy feathers, including their dramatically feathered legs, which, along with their short, single comb, make them a good fit for cold weather. Cochins come in many colors including classic buff, partridge and silver-laced. The blue variety is rare, because the blue feather gene isn't dominant, and the Frizzled Cochin, a breed with curly feathers, is even more unusual. Most varieties of cochins are bred both standard and bantam.

Size: Standard hen: 8 ½ pounds (3.85 kg); Bantam hen: 1 ¾ pounds (793 g)

Eggs: Brown

Faverolle

Faverolle

The Faverolle bloodlines are unknown, but the breed is considered a strong layer with a distinctive appearance that includes a fluffy beard and muffs, feathered legs and five toes. The well-loved Salmon Faverolle has a creamy white beard and muff, with a body, tail and wings that are more light brown than pink. The breed is considered to be gentle, and even affectionate toward the backyard farmer, though not always toward other breeds.

Size: Standard hen: 6 ½ pounds (2.7 kg)

Eggs: Brown

Silver Spangled Hamburg

Hamburg

Small, active birds, known to be good foragers and fliers, Hamburgs do best in free-range flocks. They are not unfriendly, but they are flighty and easily startled, good qualities for a free-range bird. The polka-dotted Silver Spangled Hamburg and the finely-lined Golden Penciled Hamburg are among the most common versions of the breed whose origins are unknown. (Some say the Netherlands, while others trace the breed back to Turkey.) The Hamburg is a light eater, but a strong layer of medium-sized white eggs.

Size: Standard hen: 4 pounds (1.8 kg)

Eggs: White

Single Comb Brown Leghorn

Leghorn

The lively Leghorns are specifically bred for eggs, with healthy birds laying an extra-large to jumbo egg every day and laying longer before molting than most birds. These classic-looking hens, with a single red comb, weigh about 4 pounds (1.8 kg) at maturity and begin laying at four to five months. The bright white Pearl-White Leghorn is a backyard favorite for its consistent, prolific egg production and steady, if not cuddly, temperament. The Single Comb Brown Leghorn is a colorful, chipmunk-striped version of the classic white.

Size: Standard hen: 4 ½ pounds (2 kg); Bantam hen: Just under 1 ½ pounds (680 g)

Eggs: White

Cuckoo Maran

Maran

Known for their good disposition and large, chocolate-colored eggs, Marans were developed in the French coastal town of Maran in the 1800s. The chickens are a cross between an Asiatic breed and the local French game birds, which gave the Marans their narrow feathers, strong body and short tails. Today's Marans also have the good free-ranging instincts of their game bird ancestors. The popular Cuckoo variety resemble the Barred Rock breed, with white- and slate-colored stripes.

Size: Full-size hen: About 6 pounds

Eggs: Dark brown

Buff Orpington

Orpington

The calm, affectionate Orpingtons are trendy birds for the backyard farm, especially the beautiful Buff version with golden feathers. Orpingtons were bred to be a general-purpose bird, with consistent brown-egg production. The Orpingtons' frame appears more substantial because of its full feathers, making it a good cold weather bird.

Size: Standard hen: 8 pounds (3.6 kg)

Eggs: Brown

Barred Rock

Plymouth Rock and Barred Rock

A popular breed since it was first bred from a Dominique and Black Java flock in the mid 1800s, Plymouth Rocks can be recognized by their clean yellow legs. The Barred Rock version of the breed, with yellow skin, a medium comb and a distinctive black and white striped pattern, is the most common. Baby chicks are dark gray or black with white patches. Partridge Rocks, with black and yellow beaks and a delicate brown-black feather pattern, are also popular. The breed is known for its friendliness, cold-hardiness and reliable brown-egg production.

Size: Standard hen: 7 ½ pounds (3.4 kg)

Eggs: Brown

White Crested Black Polish

Polish

Known for their unique look, the Polish breed is recognized by the large crest of feathers on the top of the head. They are not strong layers or setters and are most often bred as show birds. They are a backyard favorite due to their tame temperament and ability to liven any flock. However, they can be skittish as their abundant crest causes limited vision.

Size: Standard hen: 4 ½ pounds (2 kg)

Eggs: White

Quail Antwerp Belgian

Quail Antwerp Belgian (also know as Bearded D'Anvers)

A unique bird with a thick beard and striking spike of a tail, the gregarious Quail Antwerp Belgian has a black and straw-colored body with a brownish-yellow beard and breast. The small birds (no standard size of the breed exists) are known for their friendliness and their ability to adapt to small spaces. They are good layers, though their eggs are small, and they tend toward broodiness.

Size: Bantam hen: Just under 1 ½ pounds (680 g)

Eggs: White

Rhode Island Red

Rhode Island Red

This is one of the few breeds developed (yes, in Rhode Island) not for show, but as a good egg layer with a meaty frame that thrives in both free-range and confined flocks. This well-loved mahogany-colored bird with a single red comb is hardy, with a reputation as a prolific egg layer that rarely goes broody. They are also sometimes more focused on egg production than people. The Rhode Island White is actually a separate breed.

Size: Standard hen: 6 ½ pounds (2.9 kg); Bantam hen: Just under 2 pounds (907 g)

Eggs: Brown

White Silkie

Silkie

This bantam breed traces its history to before Marco Polo, who reported seeing this unusual bird with black skin and flesh and wild hair-like feathers during his Asian travels. Silkies, with their eye-hiding crests (the face is even more hidden on the bearded varieties), are known to be friendly and docile, making them good pets. They aren't good layers, but have a reputation for being good setters and mothers. Silkies come in many colors, including the popular white variety. As with all birds, the blue is unusual.

Size: Bantam hen: 2 pounds (907 g)

Eggs: White

Red Star

Star

Black and Red Star chickens are popular for being gentle and easy to raise with a good feed-conversion ration. That is, they produce large brown eggs consistently in both hot and cold weather for a small amount of feed. Black Star hens are black with gold hackles and breast feathers and single comb. Red Star hens are reddish brown with white flecks. Star chicks are sex-linked, meaning they can be easily and accurately sexed by color at birth.

Size: Standard hen: 6 pounds (2.7 kg)

Eggs: Brown

MURRAY MCMURRAY'S CHICKEN PROBLEM SOLVING

BACKYARD CHICKEN FARMING ISN'T WITHOUT SOME PROBLEMS, BUT THEY ARE OFTEN EASY TO SOLVE

Raising healthy chickens is typically a straight forward task, but occasionally your flock will confront you with a perplexing problem. Your best egg layer might start eating her egg or your most friendly, docile hen might become the victim of pecking. If you're observing your flock as part of your daily routine, you're likely to catch these types of problems early.

ONE OF MY CHICKENS IS PECKING AT THE OTHERS IN THE FLOCK

If one of your chickens is pecking at and injuring another (or occasionally herself), it's important to intervene quickly. The sight of blood can incite other chickens to pick at the injured bird.

Chickens might peck because they are crowded or too hot; evaluate the size of the brooder or coop and the ventilation and heat source (if you are using one). Bright light can also cause pecking, which is why red, not white, lights are recommended. A crowded feeder or waterer can also lead to pecking. Make sure there's enough room for all your chickens to eat and drink. Or your chickens might just be bored. Giving your chickens something to do, such as grass cuttings or a dust bath to play with in the run or even perches in the coop, can alleviate the pecking.

If a chicken is injured, isolate the injured bird and use topical ointment until the wounds are healed. Some ointments include ingredients that are unpalatable to chickens to discourage further pecking.

If you have a problem with pecking in your flock and none of the usual interventions work, you can trim the beak of the offending bird to prevent further injury. Using typical fingernail clippers or clippers designed for dogs, trim a small amount of beak from both sides of the top beak to blunt the sharp end. Do not trim the top beak so it is smaller than the bottom beak and do not trim the bottom beak. A hen uses its bottom beak as a shovel for food. Trimming the bottom beak would make it difficult, if not impossible, for the bird to get the nourishment it needs.

ONE OF MY CHICKENS IS EATING EGGS

Eggs taste good. The best way to prevent your chickens from eating eggs is to prevent them from ever tasting raw eggs.

Encourage your birds to lay their eggs in the nesting boxes and collect eggs every day, so that very few are accidentally broken. If an egg is broken, clean up the yolk quickly. You can add bedding to soak up the egg. And don't serve raw eggs to your birds, although hard-boiled or scrambled eggs are fine.

Backyard chicken farmers have different tactics to stop egg-eating once it starts. Some replace the collected eggs with golf balls (the same trick used to encourage hens to lay in the nesting boxes) that the bird will peck at without success. Others fill an egg with spicy mustard, which most birds dislike.

If you can identify which of your hens is the culprit, isolating her and promptly removing her eggs for several days could solve the problem. Left unchecked, however, an egg-eating hen can teach the whole flock her bad habits.

ONE OF MY HENS WON'T LEAVE THE NESTING BOX AND IS BROODING

You have a broody hen, whose hormones have told her it's time to nurture the eggs she has laid. This is natural for the hen, but not ideal for the backyard chicken farmer. A broody hen will occupy a nesting box and will stop laying eggs while she is intent on nurturing unfertilized eggs that will never hatch. That said, some backyard chicken farmers just let the chicken be broody until she gets over it.

Some breeds are more prone to broodiness, or "setting," than others and hens are more often broody in the spring, as the days lengthen. The first signs of broodiness may be excessive clucking when the hen is in the nesting box or aggressiveness if you try to remove an egg from under her in the nesting box. As with most goings-on in your coop, it's best to catch impending broodiness early and make efforts to prevent it. Once a chicken is broody, it can be hard to convince her to return to laying anytime soon.

To minimize broodiness be sure to collect eggs at least once a day, and more often if possible, so that the broody hen doesn't have any eggs to nurture. If you find the hen in the nesting box, remove her to the coop or the run each time. You can also remove or cover the nesting box that the broody hen favors, making sure there are enough nesting boxes available for the rest of the flock. Relocating the broody hen to a different coop may also help since chickens are creatures of habit.

A "broody coop" is another option. A broody coop is a hanging cage with a wire or other open floor that allows air flow under the chicken. When a hen is broody, her temperature increases to incubate the eggs; air flow helps regulate the temperature and discourages broodiness. One to three days in the broody coop will typically break a hen of broodiness, though it can take a week or more for the hen to begin laying eggs again. Another trick is to put a plastic bag filled with ice under the broody chicken each morning. This sometimes convinces the chicken to leave the nesting box.

ONE OF MY HENS ISN'T LAYING EGGS

There are many reasons why an egg-laying hen might stop laying eggs. If she isn't suffering from poor nutrition (see page 113), isn't broody (see page 165), isn't molting (see page 137) and isn't stressed (see page 93), she might be egg bound. This last condition, when a hen is unable to lay a formed egg, is a medical concern. You might notice that the hen is lethargic, with a lack of appetite and straining to lay an egg. You may even be able to feel the shape of an egg when you gently palpitate her abdomen. An egg-bound hen can die from the condition so it's important to help the hen lay the egg. Placing her in a shallow, warm bath might loosen the egg. If that doesn't work, you'll need to call a veterinarian.

ONE OF MY CHICKENS IS FLIGHTY

If you have a chicken whose flying is causing a problem, you can trim the wing feathers on one side of the body to disrupt balance in flight, thereby limiting or preventing the flying. Done correctly, this is no more painful than a haircut. The feathers will grow back. To trim the feathers, turn the bird upside down, pull one wing away from the body, fan the wing out and use sharp scissors to trim the small feathers you find there. You might want help restraining the chicken during the trim.

ONE OF MY CHICKENS MAY HAVE WORMS

Some species of worms can live in a chicken without causing any problems, but if your chicken seems ill, thin, or gaining weight slowly despite eating a lot of food, worms may be the problem. Sometimes worms can also be diagnosed by examining the chicken droppings. The most common, troublesome worm in a backyard flock is a roundworm. Treatment for worms is to deworm the whole flock with a commercial dewormer designed for chickens. Some backyard farmers deworm their flock twice a year, often in the spring and in the fall, as a precaution. Deworming medication can typically be purchased at a feed or pet store and is usually mixed with the chickens' feed or water. Some backyard farmers report success using diatomaceous earth to prevent and kill worms.

ONE OF MY CHICKENS JUST SEEMS SICK

Like the parent of a child coming down with an ear infection, an attentive backyard farmer just knows when something is off with a member of the flock. Observe your chickens daily and note if any of them seem unlike themselves. The same symptoms that make a child look sick also make a chicken look sick, such as lethargy, paleness or lack of appetite.

A sick chicken should be separated from the flock. Any eggs laid by a sick chicken should be discarded and the usual health precautions, such as washing your hands before and after handling the chicken and wearing coop-only clothing to prevent the spread of disease, should be followed. Take care of the ill chicken last as a further precaution.

If the symptoms can't be traced to hunger, dehydration, extreme temperature, worms, or the inability to lay an egg and the chicken doesn't have any visible wounds, a veterinarian may be needed.

ONE OF MY CHICKENS DIED

Even a well-cared-for chicken can die unexpectedly. It's sad, but it's also a natural part of life on a farm. If the bird died from a predator attack or simply old age, it should be removed from the coop and disposed of. Local regulation will dictate the proper method. Often, you can bury the carcass, at least three feet (92 cm) deep to deter predators, burn it or contact a veterinarian for other disposal methods. If a bird has died for unknown reasons, handle the carcass with additional care, using gloves and other sanitary precautions. If you suspect illness, a veterinarian can be helpful in identifying the cause of death and preventing other birds in your flock from suffering the same fate.

I WANT TO INTRODUCE NEW CHICKENS TO THE FLOCK

Introducing new chickens to an existing flock can be difficult. Both groups of birds already have an established pecking order and combining the groups will disrupt that. Bullying and pecking might occur as a new pecking order is established.

If you plan to introduce new chickens to your flock, wait until they are grown and can fend for themselves in the coop. It's also best to introduce a group of chickens, not just one or two, into the flock at the same time. Chickens of the same breed may integrate into the flock more easily. Physical differences like a big crest can lead to pecking.

Be sure that your coop has enough space for more birds and consider installing at least two waterers and feeders so that the birds can avoid one another if they want to. Other tips from backyard chicken farmers include locating the birds side by side in separate coops for a while so they can see, but not attack one another, or placing the new chickens into the coop at night while the flock is sleeping, to avoid stress.

Observe your newly combined flock carefully and be ready to intervene quickly if problems arise between the chickens.

About the Authors

For almost a century, Murray McMurray Hatchery has been a friend to the backyard chicken farmer, shipping millions of healthy chicks and all the equipment necessary to raise a happy flock from Webster City, Iowa, to chicken lovers in all 50 states. The Murray McMurray Method for raising chickens in five minutes a day is based on knowledge gained over decades of experience with chickens and first-time chicken farmers. Murray McMurray Hatchery president Bud Wood and his team – especially hatchery staff Curt McCoskey, Kent Barnefuss, Debbie Jaycox and Chris Huseman and farmer Bob Nilles – shared their collective chicken wit and wisdom for this book. Learn more about Murray McMurray Hatchery and its thriving community of backyard chicken farmers at mcmurrayhatchery.com.

Index